THE UNCOMMON SPEECH OF PARADISE

THE UNCOMMON SPEECH
OF PARADISE

Poems on the Art of Poetry

Edited by Robert Hedin and James Lenfestey

WHITE PINE PRESS / BUFFALO, NEW YORK

White Pine Press
P.O. Box 236
Buffalo, NY 14201
www.whitepine.org

Publication of this book was supported by public funds from the New York
State Council on the Arts, with the support of Governor Andrew M. Cuomo
and the New York State Legislature, a State Agency.

Acknowledgments and copyright information begin on page 237.

Printed and bound in the United States of America.

Cover image: Odile Redon, *Centaur with Cello,* oil on canvas, 1910.

ISBN 978-1-945680-48-9

Library of Congress Control Number: 2020952141

Not 'common speech'
a dead level
but the uncommon speech of paradise,
tongue in which oracles
speak to beggars and pilgrims:

not illusion but what Whitman called
'the path
between reality and the soul,'
a language
excelling itself to be itself,

speech akin to the light
with which at day's end and day's
renewal, mountains
sing to each other across the cold valleys.

Denise Levertov
from "A Common Ground"

Contents

V - All This Fiddle

VI - The Real Work

VI - Lines Stitching Here to There

VIII - Letters to the World

THE UNCOMMON SPEECH OF PARADISE

FOREWORD

"We hail what heals, sponsors, restores."
— Gwendolyn Brooks

The Uncommon Speech of Paradise highlights the works of 120 modern and contemporary poets from seventeen countries, presenting a wide variety of voices, styles, and perspectives on the theory, practice, and purpose of poetry.

Horace wrote the first poem we know of on the art of poetry, "Ars Poetica," during the Pax Romana in the first century B.C.E. Horace's chatty hexameters instruct poets and readers alike on the why, how, and wherefore of poetry. Liu Chi's prose poem, "Wen Fu," performs a similar task for Chinese lyric poetry in the third century C.E. *The Uncommon Speech of Paradise* carries on the spirit of Horace's "Ars Poetica" and Liu Chi's "Wen Fu," allowing the poets themselves to speak through their poems about the art they practice, not in their own defense but in embodiment— that huge Latinate word Robert Frost used when he could not find another to describe the arrival of the Unknowable.

In doing so, they address fundamental questions of the art. What is poetry? Why does it matter? To whom does it speak? What does Szymborska say, and MacLeish and Sexton and Lux, not in essays but in poems themselves? What do Olds, Mueller, and Hampl say about why they turned to poetry in the first place? What do Troupe, Pastan, Bly, and Collins say about form? What does the muse say about the muse?

The Uncommon Speech of Paradise can be read as a sustained dialogue, poets speaking back and forth through their poems in often spirited ways as a tutorial on poetic practice and purpose. Behind each of their poems is the undeniable conviction that poetry enriches lives, that it gives voice to the yearnings of the spirit, and offers readers insights into who we are, where we have come from, our values and aspirations. Ultimately, they come together to create not a conversation so much as a chorus, revealing a universal, human desire to connect. June Jordan writes:

These words
they are stones in the water rippling away

These skeletal lines
they are desperate arms for my longing and love.
I am a stranger
learning to worship the strangers
around me

whoever you are
whatever I may become.

Robert McKee, in his remarkable book, *Story*, opens with a brilliant argument for the compelling, inherent human need for stories. But people have also always needed, and practiced, prayer. And music. And for well over 2,500 years the coming together of both, which is poetry.

Poetry is much more like prayer than storytelling and, like prayer, it can be rambling, unfocused, pleading, unfair, inward, even silent. But it always reaches past prose toward music, just as the sutras and psalms are not God, but pleas, a beseeching. Poetry, Horace said in comparing poetry to beekeeping, is "sweetness and light." But he didn't say it is honey. Because poetry, like prose, like speech, is syllables—phonemes, "tiny sound particles" in Robert Bly's more felicitous phrase—common to all in a language group, which is why it is mistakenly yoked with prose and speech. But music is the closer analogy.

The closest approximation of the sound of the human soul may be a bow drawn across a cello's strings. That pure vibrating sound strums the dark cavern of being, vibrates the core, makes one ecstatic, makes one weep. Poetry does that too, "as if the top of my head were taken off," as Emily Dickinson asks of poems. In this way poetry and music are similar, and why seven of the nine muses of Greek tradition represent poetry and music. What the cello says, what it vibrates, is unsayable. Yet, poets say it every day. Read a novel to hang breathless with the journey. Read a poem and weep now or cry out with ecstatic discovery.

Employing the powerful and intimate tool of language, poets practice their art at the studio desk or chair or on the subway or mountaintop. They do so not for recognition, not for vocation, nor for praise, but because poetry is the best way to express the astonishing facts of their inner lives and outer confusions and encounters with beauty. Painters are infected by light, sculptors with light and touch, poets with the sound and sense of syllables seeking to capture the soul's emanations.

Perhaps, as some have said, we are all poets and don't know it. Meaning, of course, that all humans have the miracle of language in their mouths, an organized concert of sound. Wendell Berry writes:

> The first man who whistled
> thought he had a wren in his mouth.
> He went around all day
> with his lips puckered,
> afraid to swallow.

"Language is fossil poetry," Ralph Waldo Emerson wrote. Poets, more than other artists, pay acute attention to the magical layers of these fossil sound particles, to their arrangements and rhythms and the pauses between, in the same way musicians count notes and rests. "It is not metres," Emerson added, "but metre-making argument that makes a poem—a thought so passionate and alive that, like the spirit of a plant or an animal, it has an architecture of its own, and adorns nature with a new thing."

The Uncommon Speech of Paradise is divided into eight sections, each highlighting an essential aspect of the poem-making process. The book champions no particular poetics. Instead, its embrace is wide. Some of the selections are readily identifiable and still enjoy popularity today. Others are not well-known, and some will be introduced to readers for the first time.

Ultimately, *The Uncommon Speech of Paradise* celebrates what Emily Dickinson calls the "Possibility"—for the poet, the reader, the listener, the dreamer, the penitent—to be swept away, upstream or down. The result is an abundance of eloquence that will not fail readers in their quest to understand the mysterious flow of art, and maybe, just maybe, of what we call existence.

—James Lenfestey and Robert Hedin

I.
In the Beginning

How a single word
may shimmer and rise
off the page, a wafer of
syllabic light, a bulb
of glowing meaning,
whatever the word,
try "tempestuous"or "suffer,"
any word you have held
or traded so it lives a new life
the size of two worlds. . .

Naomi Shihab Nye
from "Vocabulary of Dearness"

Gary Snyder (1930–   )

RIPRAP

Lay down these words
Before your mind like rocks.
      placed solid, by hands
In choice of place, set
Before the body of the mind
      in space and time:
Solidity of bark, leaf, or wall
      riprap of things:
Cobble of milky way,
      straying planets,
These poems, people,
      lost ponies with
Dragging saddles—
      and rocky sure-foot trails.
The worlds like an endless
      four-dimensional
Game of Go.
      ants and pebbles
In the thin loam, each rock a word
      a creek-washed stone
Granite: ingrained
      with torment of fire and weight
Crystal and sediment linked hot
      all change, in thoughts,
As well as things.

William Carlos Williams (1883–1963)

A SORT OF A SONG

Let the snake wait under
his weed
and the writing
be of words, slow and quick, sharp
to strike, quiet to wait,
sleepless.

—through metaphor to reconcile
the people and the stones.
Compose. (No ideas
but in things) Invent!
Saxifrage is my flower that splits
the rocks.

Alberto Ríos (1952–   )

AN INSTRUCTION TO MYSELF

Shepherd the things of the world to the page
But the things themselves   Not just their names
which represent them which are their lawyers
The things of the world themselves   Rouse them
to us as once they roused you so much you cannot
forget or leave or ignore them   Give us this
fitfulness both burden and gift   This glint that
haunts us pushes us into dream   Into the great
prairies the green and gray seas the unbearable
deserts the boundless bird-sky of imagination
This song, this great song   Our hands our fingers
our muscles making translation of every-
thing into its most fragile vessel   Into word

Rita Dove (1952–)

Ö

Shape the lips to an *o*, say *a*.
That's *island*.

One word of Swedish has changed the whole neighborhood.
When I look up, the yellow house on the corner
is a galleon stranded in flowers. Around it

the wind. Even the high roar of a leaf-mulcher
could be the horn-blast from a ship
as it skirts the misted shoals.

We don't need much more to keep things going.
Families complete themselves
and refuse to budge from the present,
the present extends its glass forehead to sea
(backyard breezes, scattered cardinals)

and if, one evening, the house on the corner
took off over the marshland,
neither I nor my neighbor
would be amazed. Sometimes

a word is found so right it trembles
at the slightest explanation.
You start out with one thing, end
up with another, and nothing's
like it used to be, not even the future.

Joyce Sutphen (1949–   )

IT'S AMAZING

Another word for that is astonishing
or astounding, remarkable or marvelous.

It's also slightly startling, which leads to
shocking and upsetting, perhaps a bit

disquieting, and that is troubling and
distressing—you could say outrageous

and deplorable, which leads to wicked
and more precise equations such as

sinful and immoral or just plain bad
and wrong. It's amazing, which is just to say

bewildering and unexpected, that
it happened out of the blue, and that we went

all the way from miraculous to absurd,
within the syllables of just one word.

Anne Sexton (1928–1974)

WORDS

Be careful of words,
even the miraculous ones.
For the miraculous we do our best,
sometimes they swarm like insects
and leave not a sting but a kiss.
They can be as good as fingers.
They can be as trusty as the rock
you stick your bottom on.
But they can be both daisies and bruises.

Yet I am in love with words.
They are doves falling out of the ceiling.
They are six holy oranges sitting in my lap.
They are the trees, the legs of summer,
and the sun, its passionate face.

Yet often they fail me.
I have so much I want to say,
so many stories, images, proverbs, etc.
But the words aren't good enough,
the wrong ones kiss me.
Sometimes I fly like an eagle
but with the wings of a wren.

But I try to take care
and be gentle to them.
Words and eggs must be handled with care.
Once broken they are impossible
things to repair.

Franny Choi (1989–)

WE USED OUR WORDS WE USED
WHAT WORDS WE HAD

we used our words we used what words we had
to weld, what words we had we wielded, kneeled,
we knelt. & wept we wrung the wet the sweat
we wracked our lips we rang for words to ward
off sleep to warn to want ourselves, to want
the earth we mouthed it wound our vowels until
it fit, in fits the earth we mounted roused
& rocked we harped we yawned & tried to yawp
& tried to fix, affixed, we facted, felt.
we fattened fanfared anthemed hammered, felt
the words' worth stagnate, snap in half in heat
the wane the melt what words we'd hoarded halved
& holey, porous, meanwhile tide still tide.
& we: still washed for sounds to mark. & marked.

Mona Sa'udi (1945–)

WHY DON'T I WRITE

Why don't I write in the language of air? master a new tongue
    with a different taste, a language that dances,
that goes drunk through the streets, embraces trees, walks
    on water. . . that cries? a language
that burns the world, and gathers autumn leaves?
If I tell the sea to become a word—will the sea consent?
If I tell the word to die, if I pile up the words of the ages
past, present, and future, and say to the sun:
    Burn heaps of words
and say to the earth: Bury the ashes of words
and say to the ashes: Word-ashes
bring forth a sorcerer's tongue
    to tell fire: Be word
    and word: Be a poem
without words,
which can neither be read, nor seen, nor heard.

Translated from the Arabic by Kamal Boullata

W. S. Merwin (1927–2019)

THE UNWRITTEN

Inside this pencil
crouch words that have never been written
never been spoken
never been taught

they're hiding

they're awake in there
dark in the dark
hearing us
but they won't come out
not for love not for time not for fire

even when the dark has worn away
they'll still be there
hiding in the air
multitudes in days to come may walk through them
breathe them
be none the wiser

what script can it be
that they won't unroll
in what language
would I recognize it
would I be able to follow it
to make out the real names
of everything

maybe there aren't
many
it could be that there's only one word
and it's all we need

it's here in this pencil

every pencil in the world
is like this

Richard Foerster (1949–)

EARLY AND LATE

1

Southpawed, I sat in St. Brendan's first-grade class,
at a wrought-framed desk, hands primly folded
atop the gouged, graffitoed hardwood lid that bore
the dark veneer of all the other straight-backed,
uniformed boys who'd passed that way before.

Too unschooled for pens, I'd set my fat, blunt-leaded
pencil in its shallow trough, the red shaft scarred
with the pit-marks of teething. All black and white
against the chalked blackboard, Sister taught
the rigid curves and angularities of early ABCs,

but I, true to some time-tested prejudice,
was the sinister recalcitrant, her only devil-
handed boy she placed, cowed and cowering,
closest to her desk so that when my left hand
would reach, by instinct, for that instrument of self-

expression, I'd feel her wooden knuckle-raps and bear
my red Fs home. How many pencils did I sharpen
into extinction, practicing what seemed a secret code
I longed to break, enjoined as I was—though I couldn't
grasp it then—in the ardor of apprenticeship?

2

What flows now between the mind-
forged nib and the paper's pure
vacancy: these vagrant trails,

31

blue-black as night, stipped
with distant glimmer, jots
and tittles, the deep dye

of being, cursive, connected,
stroked, and curled, the flourish
of a word—there!—like a whip

inked into meaning.

Jack Gilbert (1925–2012)

THE FORGOTTEN DIALECT OF THE HEART

How astonishing it is that language can almost mean,
And frightening that it does not quite. *Love*, we say.
God, we say, *Rome* and *Michiko*, we write, and the words
get it wrong. We say *bread* and it means according
to which nation. French has no word for home,
and we have no word for strict pleasure. A people
In northern India is dying out because their ancient
tongue has no words for endearment. I dream of lost
vocabularies that might express some of what
we no longer can. Maybe the Etruscan texts would
finally explain why the couples on their tombs
are smiling. And maybe not. When the thousands
of mysterious Sumerian tablets were translated,
they seemed to be business records. But what if they
are poems or psalms? My joy is the same as twelve
Ethiopian goats standing silent in the morning light.
0 Lord, thou are slabs of salt and ingots of copper,
As grand as ripe barley lithe under the wind's labor.
Her breasts are six white oxen loaded with bolts
Of long-fibered Egyptian cotton. My love is a hundred
pitchers of honey. Shiploads of thuya are what
My body wants to say to your body. Giraffes are this
desire in the dark. Perhaps the spiral Minoan script
Is not language but a map. What we feel most has
no name but amber, archers, cinnamon horses, and birds.

Linda Hogan (1947–   )

FIRST LANGUAGE: SANDHILL CRANES

Here the water is different every moment.
It is a place with everything changing,
even the sounds.
Some call these birds the changers of language,
the tellers of stories.
I say they were here on the first day of sky creation
when one of our many gods said or thought,
Let there be infinite sky
and creatures with wings,
the red of setting sun
over a golden eye
as if to disguise what is seen.
And now at night all of the birds settle low in the dark water,
as if believing they are hidden away
for the night
they will be
tall ones standing now and then
noisy and singing,
talking, looking for a mate.
All night new ones arrive
from the four directions,
the horizon
as if coming up from the ground
and not down from the sky,
these the long neck of this planet
crying out. They are the ancient beginnings.
Here they come. Listen.
Coming near to us,
gathering,
standing close to us,
speaking out to us
all together,

34

this island of crane,
all one mind,
altogether
speaking
our first language.

Francisco Aragón (1968–)

POEM WITH CITATIONS FROM THE O.E.D.

First *voz* because I recall the taste
of beans wrapped in a corn
tortilla—someone brings it
to me, retrieves what's left
on the plate, the murmured vowels

taking root, taking hold—mi
lengua materna. Then later learn
another spelling, label the "box"
where sound's produced, draw, too,
the tongue, the teeth, the lips. *The voyce*

that is dysposid to songe and melody
hath thyse proprytees: smalle,
subtyll, thicke, clere, sharpe...
in thirteen ninety-eight. But what
of the deaf-mute, his winning shout

—BINGO!—knocking me over?
Huxley noted: *voice may exist*
without speech and speech may exist
without voice. The first time I spoke
with my father was on the phone, so his

was all I had to go on: that,
and what he'd say—things he'd hear
"inside." In *Doctor's Dilemma*
Shaw wrote: *When my patients*
tell me they hear voices
I lock them up. The pitch, the tone, the range:
a way of trying to know him. Now hers
and his are in the pages of a book:

Un baile de máscaras by Sergio
Ramirez, his characters echoing

words, rhythms I heard
until she died, hearing them as well
for months after—whenever I spoke
with him. *Who hath not shared that calm*
so still and deep, The voiceless thought

which would not speak but weep.

Heid Erdrich (1963–   )

OFFERING: WORDS

*Gichimookomaanimo: speaks American, speaks
the Long Knives' language*

Mother, if you look it up, is *source*,
(fount and fountainhead—origin,
provenance and provenience,
root) and *wellspring*.
Near her in the dictionary you will find
we all spring *mother-naked*,
(bare, stripped, unclothed, undressed, and raw)
with nothing but *mother-wit*
(brains, brain-power, sense) our *native wit*
with which we someday might *mother*,
(nurse, care for, serve, and wait on)
if we don't first look it up and discover
the fullness of its meaning.

Such interesting language, this *tongue*,
(our diction, idiom, speech, and vernacular)
also *sign language*,
(gesture language)
and *contact language*,
which was English or Ojibwe,
either way; both spoke forward our *mother country*,
our *motherland* (see also fatherland,
our home, our homeland, our land)
called *soil* in English our *mother tongue*,
our *native language* that is not my *Native language*
not the *mother language* Ojibwe:
wellspring of many tongues, nurse, origin, and source.

38

Julia Alvarez (1950–   )

I, TOO, SING AMERICA

I know it's been said before
but not in this voice
of the plátano
and the mango,
marimba y bongó,
not in this sancocho
of inglés
con español.

Ay, sí,
it's my turn
to oh say
what I see,
I'm going to sing America!
with all América
inside me:
from the soles
of Tierra del Fuego
to the thin waist
of Chiriquí
up the spine of the Mississippi
through the heartland
of the Yanquis
To the great plain face of Canada—
all of us
singing America,
the whole hemispheric
familia
belting our canción,
singing our brown skin
into that white
and red and blue song—

the big song
that sings
all America,
el canto
que cuenta
con toda América:
un *new song!*
Ya llegró el memento,
our moment
under the sun—
ese sol *that shines*
on everyone.

So, hit it maestro!
give us that Latin beat,
¡Uno-dos-tres!
One-two-three!
Ay sí,
(y bilingually):
Yo también soy América
I, too, am America.

Victor Hernández Cruz (1949–   )

LUNEQUISTICOS

In what language do you jump off one boat
to get to another one to buy something cold
to drink while at the same time you contemplate
The shapes and curves of the eyes the various
family trees have produced in all the people
present buying something cold to drink
The shades of minds each beaming glaze of their
spirit all being here for a second of my questions
I am in the young woman's tenor her lips drum
pictures of thin Spanish fans waving
Ships sailing in pictures hanging on living
room walls   Chaotic room of thirsty tongues
Moving my whistle sounds to investigate
Each glassy eyes my windows
Their fires in the cold drinks
So if I ask you my creature friends in what language
do I ask the question to come in: Do I take my
Oye/lo/que/one/time/eva/or/iva/decir/que/uno/una
ves/sepuso/la/cosa/de bullets/peor que/one guerra
en/the/escuela/corner/de/maestros/ya/con/lisencia
y/todo/una/mes/mass/de/masas/tambien/con/masa/cuando
ella/pasaba/lo/profesores/le/cantaban/siquere/gozar
ben/a/bailar/tengo/libros/de/to/colores/estudiaremos
el/at/most/fear/el/turn/de/una/language/como/hace/in
side/the/mind/calculate/while/it/separates/words/in/two
languages/sounds/spellings/systems/whole/tone/latitude
and/altitude/altiduego of voces/in/gas/communications/gets
filtered/and/ironed/tambien/the/two/musics/through/one/breath
Para/
    Or do I spray it around in straight talk
Filtar: Presuming you tailored the rough edges of your

41

tenor dress it up with my wave of syllables say to me
What is your idea what flavor did you ask for
In what tense does it remain the same color when it
laughs in your cup.
Pure orange juice.
Pure ginger root-boiled
Pure grapefruit—the ones with freckles.
Pure Spanish/Pure English
Pure tunes tos tono tos tones
When is exactly Saturday and Sabado two different nights
Do you say in one aspect of the night your deep feelings
to whoever might be involved in a need to hear them from
you or do you avoid what's really going on and talk other
heavens go over to the jukebox before ordering a cold
drink put on Tito Rodriquez's "Double Talk" put the boat
In reverse and relax you have just given birth to twins
The tongue figures out how not to jump from one boat to
another and takes a dash out onto the street where the
wrong speed can brake anybody's record.

Sandra M. Castillo (1962–   )

LETTER TO YENI
ON PEERING INTO HER LIFE

I see you, not as you stand before me,
so full of language threatening to spill from you,
a silver-blue luminous substance the page of cups
might carry in love, in a gold chalice,
but as a child I might have seen, held,
had I been an adult on that island
where we might have become anyone
other than ourselves.

You are a sound you say your father carries,
a beat in the heart of an African drum
that seduced him with the thunder of *Changó*
the red of blood and earth,
a flesh-pink guava growing inside you,
its seeds on the tips of your fingers
like islands, like memories becoming leaves,
their veined undersides becoming maps,
palmlines, bridges where the sound of water collects childhood
in a blue bucket of memory,
where my Tio Machuco stands with childhood sandwiches I ate
sitting on the cold terraza, leaning against the Southwest red
of that couch Tia Hilda discarded like a useless memory
when we were no longer voices in open rooms with connecting
    doors,
when we were words, onion-skinned paper
as transparent as re-written history or exile.

Albert Goldbarth (1948–   )

BEFORE

The class was History, that's
what I wanted—the bridge
the bent Yid ragman took reluctantly
between steamship and sweatshop, or
older than that: the landbridge
something almost a horse was
grazing its way to Alaska
across on something almost hooves,
or older: something almost a leg
that was the grayveined print of a leg
in a web, before a bridge could be anything
more than a body's own
furthest extension. I was
seventeen. It was sunny. I'd come
from History, and before that
from a lineage of ragpickers,
songpluckers, kettlemenders, renderers
of humpfat for the candles, masters of
disputation over a nuance of scripture,
debtors, diddlers, elegiasts and jewelers
—history too, though the textbook
didn't say it. The page said Presidents
and paper. I wanted something from
before paper—wasps,
the fluted home of their making.
I wanted the first bone
of my bones. I wanted the word
before the alphabet, the word like a suckstone
working up spit. And then I stopped,
near Washtenaw and Ainslie, on the bridge
above the sewerage ditch, and sun
as if meeting a challenge made the stars

of a constellation-story burn
that urban rut's otherwise lustreless
flow. It was the sign of The Cart,
and there too, in the story, sun
bedazzled dull surfaces: all those heaps
of garment-district scraps he peddled,
a few abused tin pots, and who knows
how or why but some wholeskinned Spanish onions,
wool socks, and a single tired rose. I
still remember this: his humming something
tuneless, as if from before the idea of song
took full root in American soil—but
like the rose, though it drooped, though maybe
the worm ate in it, his song was handsome,
a lady would accept it and understand. And
this: my face was reflected, wavery
but ascertainably wide-eyed, on his pots.
Or in the sewerage currents—and then the
stars shifted, light was
sun again, and I was something almost
a man, on its way home,
humming its wanting. I was a boy
with a book. And this was long before
I'd learn to have words for what I wanted,
but what I wanted was something
like a bottle with a notepage in it,
thrown to sea—the clarity of glass,
but from before glass; and the urgency
of that written note, before writing.
—Maybe the water itself,
the message its salt.

Nuala Ní Dhomhnaill (1952–)

THE LANGUAGE ISSUE

I place my hope on the water
in this little boat
of the language, the way a body might put
an infant

in a basket of intertwined
iris leaves,
its underside proofed
with bitumen and pitch,

then set the whole thing down amidst
the sedge
and bulrushes by the edge
of a river

only to have it borne hither and thither,
not knowing where it might end up;
in the lap, perhaps,
of some Pharaoh's daughter.

Translated from the Irish by Paul Muldoon

Linda Gregg (1942–2019)

SEARCHING FOR THE POEM

I.
The boat of the bible was
pushed into the reeds. Our chanting
is the stolen property of the sea.
Bathing is our clothing, is the mountain
I see in you. I walk up in the heat
to remember its weight. Which has
something to do with it. We are struck
dumb by what we call truth.
Having to match the foreignness of stone.
Our speech is far from the click
and shift of broken glass, making
the new colored pictures we try
to memorize in our sleep.
We are strengthened even by defeat,
honoring most what is strangest among us.

II.
I'm standing with a tree while
the sun rises, proud of the night.
She pushed the infant into the reeds
to keep the secret. Using language
for imitation. To keep the mountain
of the beloved. I walk up the mountain
in the heat to know belief. The glass
image shifts and clicks in our sleep.
Changes into another mystery
to turn the pages.

III.
The thing we are trying to say
is in the language of leaves.

We take our chanting from the sea
and clothe ourselves in the instruments
of water. We can never speak
its language. In the book they made
a boat of our reeds to hide
the child. We go down and forth,
proud to live with the night.
We walk up the mountain to relearn
the weight. To keep inside the beloved.
When we sleep the universe shifts
and clicks. We memorize each
new image and hide it for safety.
For our chanting. Get as close as possible
without knowing. Draw it with a stick.

II.
Away from the World

Grandfather
advised me:
learn a trade.
I learned
to sit at a desk
and condense.
No layoff
from this
condensery.

Lorine Niedecker
"Condensery"

T. S. Eliot (1888–1965)

from EAST COKER

So here I am, in the middle way, having had twenty years—
Twenty years largely wasted, the years of *l'entre deux guerres*
Trying to learn to use words, and every attempt
Is a wholly new start, and a different kind of failure
Because one has only learnt to get the better of words
For the thing one no longer has to say, or the way in which
One is no longer disposed to say it. And so each venture
Is a new beginning, a raid on the inarticulate
With shabby equipment always deteriorating
In the general mess of imprecision of feeling,
Undisciplined squads of emotion. And what there is to conquer
By strength and submission, has already been discovered
Once or twice, or several times, by men whom one cannot hope
To emulate—but there is no competition—
There is only the fight to recover what has been lost
And found and lost again and again: and now, under conditions
That seem unpropitious. But perhaps neither gain nor loss.
For us, there is only the trying. The rest is not our business.

Adrienne Rich (1929–2012)

from ORIGINS AND HISTORY OF CONSCIOUSNESS

Night-life. Letters, journals, bourbon
sloshed in the glass. Poems crucified on the wall,
dissected, their bird-wings severed
like trophies. No one lives in this room
without living through some kind of crisis.

No one lives in this room
without confronting the whiteness of the wall
behind the poems, planks of books,
photographs of dead heroines.
Without contemplating last and late
the true nature of poetry. The drive
to connect. The dream of a common language.

Thinking of lovers, their blind faith, their
experienced crucifixions,
my envy is not simple. I have dreamed of going to bed
as walking into clear water ringed by a snowy wood
white as cold sheets, thinking, *I'll freeze in there.*
My bare feet are numbed already by the snow
but the water
is mild, I sink and float
like a warm amphibious animal
that has broken the net, has run
through fields of snow leaving no print;
this water washes off the scent—
You are clear now
of the hunter, the trapper
the wardens of the mind—

yet the warm animal dreams on
of another animal
swimming under the snow-flecked surface of the pool,
and wakes, and sleeps again.

No one sleeps in this room without
the dream of a common language.

Ted Hughes (1930–1998)

THE THOUGHT-FOX

I imagine this midnight moment's forest:
Something else is alive
Beside the clock's loneliness
And this blank page where my fingers move.

Through the window I see no star;
Something more near
Though deeper within darkness
Is entering the loneliness:

Cold, delicately as the dark snow
A fox's nose touches, twig, leaf;
Two eyes serve a movement, that now
And again now, and now, and now

Sets neat prints into the snow
Between trees, and warily a lame
Shadow lags by stump and in hollow
Of a body that is bold to come

Across clearings, an eye,
A widening deepening greenness,
Brilliantly, concentratedly,
Coming about its own business

Till, with a sudden sharp hot stink of fox,
It enters the dark hole of the head.
The window is starless still; the clock ticks,
The page is printed.

Seamus Heaney (1939–2013)

DIGGING

Between my finger and my thumb
The squat pen rests; snug as a gun.

Under my window, a clean rasping sound
When the spade sinks into gravelly ground:
My father, digging. I look down

Till his straining rump among the flowerbeds
Bends low, comes up twenty years away
Stooping in rhythm through potato drills
Where he was digging.

The coarse boot nestled on the lug, the shaft
Against the inside knee was levered firmly.
He rooted out tall tops, buried the bright edge deep
To scatter new potatoes that we picked
Loving their cool hardness in our hands.

By God, the old man could handle a spade.
Just like his old man.

My grandfather cut more turf in a day
Than any other man on Toner's bog.
Once I carried him milk in a bottle
Corked sloppily with paper. He straightened up
To drink it, then fell to right away
Nicking and slicing neatly, heaving sods
Over his shoulder, going down and down
For the good turf. Digging.

The cold smell of potato mould, the squelch and slap
Of soggy peat, the curt cuts of an edge

Through living roots awaken in my head.
But I've no spade to follow men like them.

Between my finger and my thumb
The squat pen rests.
I'll dig with it.

Gerald Stern (1925–   )

MAKING THE LIGHT COME

My pen was always brown or blue, with stripes
of gold or silver at the shaft for streaks
of thought and feeling. I always wore the nib
on the left side. I was a mirror right-hander,
not a crazy twisted left-handed cripple,
trying to live in this world, his wrist half broken,
his shoulder shot through with pain. I lived by smiling,
I turned my face to the light—a frog does that,
not only a bird—and changed my metal table
three or four times. I struggled for rights to the sun
not only because of the heat. I wanted to see
the shadows on the wall, the trees and vines,
and I wanted to see the white wisteria
hanging from the roof. To sit half under it.
Light was my information. I was an immigrant
Jew in Boston, I was a Vietnamese
in San Jose, taking a quick lunch hour,
reading Browning—how joyous—I was worshiping
light three dozen years ago, it led me
astray, I never saw it was a flower
and darkness was the seed; I never potted
the dirt and poured the nutriments, I never
waited week after week for the smallest gleam.
I sit in the sun forgiving myself; I know
exactly when to dig. What other poet
is on his knees in the frozen clay with a spade
and a silver fork, fighting the old maples,
scattering handfuls of gypsum and moss, still worshiping?

Robert Bly (1926–   )

WORDS RISING
for Richard Eberhart

I open my journal, write a few
Words with green ink, and suddenly
Fierceness enters me, stars
Begin to revolve, and pick up
Alligator dust from under the ocean.
Writing vowels, I feel the bushy
Tail of the Great Bear
Reach down and brush the seafloor.

All those deaths we lived in the sunlit
Shelves of the Dordogne, the thousand
Tunes we sang to the skeletons
Of Papua, and all those times
We died—wounded—under the cloak
Of an animal's sniffing, all these moments
Return, and the grassy nights when
We ran in the moonlight for hours.

Watery syllables come welling
Up. When a man or woman
Feeds a few words with private grief,
The shame we knew before we could
Invent the wheel, then words grow.
The old earth-fragrance remains
In the word "and." We experience
"The" in its lonely suffering.

We are bees then; our honey is language.
Now the honey lies stored in caves
Beneath us, and the sound of words
Carries what we have forgotten.

We see a million hands with dusty
Palms turned up inside each
Verb. And there are eternal vows
Held inside the word "Jericho."

Blessings then on the man who labors
In his room writing stanzas on the lamb.
And blessings on the woman who picks the brown
Seeds of solitude in afternoon light
Out of the black seeds of loneliness.
Blessings on the dictionary maker, huddled
Among his bearded words and on the setter of songs
Who sleeps at night inside his violin case.

Ursula Le Guin (1929–2018)

from COMING OF AGE

This old notebook I write in was my father's;
he never wrote in it. A grey man,
all my lifetime, with a short grey beard,
a slight man, not tall.
The other day I saw five elephants,
big elephants, with palm-trunk legs
and continents of sides, and one,
the biggest one, had bent tusks bound
about with brass. They were waiting,
patient, to be let outside
into the sunlight and the autumn air,
moving about their stall so quietly,
using the grace of great size and the gentleness,
swaying a little, silent, strong as ships.
That was a great pleasure, to see that.
And he would have liked to see the big one
            making water,
too, like a steaming river,
enough to float ten bigots in.
O there is nothing like sheer Quantity,
mountains, elephants, minds.

Li-Young Lee (1957–   )

IN HIS OWN SHADOW

He is seated in the first darkness
of his body sitting in the lighter dark
of the room,

the greater light of day behind him,
beyond the windows, where
Time is the country.

His body throws two shadows:
One onto the table
and the piece of paper before him,
and one onto his mind.

One makes it difficult for him to see
the words he's written and crossed out
on the paper. The other
keeps him from recognizing
another master than Death. He squints.
He reads: *Does the first light hide
inside the first dark?*

He reads: *While all bodies share
the same fate, all voices do not.*

Dorianne Laux (1952–   )

DUST

Someone spoke to me last night,
told me the truth. Just a few words,
but I recognized it.
I knew I should make myself get up,
write it down, but it was late,
and I was exhausted from working
all day in the garden, moving rocks.
Now, I remember only the flavor—
not like food, sweet or sharp.
More like a fine powder, like dust.
And I wasn't elated or frightened,
but simply rapt, aware.
That's how it is sometimes—
God comes to your window,
all bright light and black wings,
and you're just too tired to open it.

Denise Levertov (1923–1997)

WRITING IN THE DARK

It's not difficult.
Anyway, it's necessary.

Wait till morning, and you'll forget.
And who knows if morning will come.

Fumble for the light, and you'll be
stark awake, but the vision
will be fading, slipping
out of reach.

You must have paper at hand,
a felt-tip pen—ballpoints don't always flow,
pencil points tend to break. There's nothing
shameful in that much prudence: those are your tools.

Never mind about crossing your t's, dotting your i's—
but take care not to cover
one word with the next. Practice will reveal
how one hand instinctively comes to the aid of the other
to keep each line
clear of the next.

Keep writing in the dark:
a record of the night; or
words that pulled you from depths of unknowing,
words that flew through your mind, strange birds
crying their urgency with human voices,

or opened
as flowers of a tree that blooms
only once in a lifetime:

words that may have the power
to make the sun rise again.

Mary Oliver (1935–2019)

AT GREAT POND

At Great Pond
the sun, rising,
scrapes his orange breast
on the thick pines,

and down tumble
a few orange feathers into
the dark water.
On the far shore

a white bird is standing
like a white candle—
or a man, in the distance,
in the clasp of some meditation—

while all around me the lilies
are breaking open again
from the black cave
of the night.

Later, I will consider
what I have seen—
what it could signify—
what words of adoration I might

make of it, and to do this
I will go indoors to my desk—
I will sit in my chair—
I will look back

into the lost morning
in which I am moving, now,
like a swimmer,
so smoothly,

so peacefully,
I am almost the lily—
almost the bird vanishing over the water
on its sleeves of light.

Stanley Kunitz (1905–2006)

THE ROUND

Light splashed this morning
on the shell-pink anemones
swaying on their tall stems;
down blue-spiked veronica
light flowed in rivulets
over the humps of the honeybees;
this morning I saw light kiss
the silk of the roses
in their second flowering,
my late bloomers
flushed with their brandy.
A curious gladness shook me.

So I have shut the doors of my house,
so I have trudged downstairs to my cell,
so I am sitting in semi-dark
hunched over my desk
with nothing for a view
to tempt me
but a bloated compost heap,
steamy old stinkpile,
under my window;
and I pick my notebook up
and I start to read aloud
the still-wet words I scribbled
on the blotted page:
"Light splashed..."

I can scarcely wait till tomorrow
when a new life begins for me,
as it does each day,
as it does each day.

Raymond Carver (1938–1988)

AT LEAST

I want to get up early one more morning,
before sunrise. Before the birds, even.
I want to throw cold water on my face
and be at my work table
when the sky lightens and smoke
begins to rise from the chimneys
of the other houses.
I want to see the waves break
on this rocky beach, not just hear them
break as I did all night in my sleep.
I want to see again the ships
that pass through the Strait from every
seafaring country in the world—
old, dirty freighters just barely moving along,
and the swift new cargo vessels
painted every color under the sun
that cut the water as they pass.
I want to keep an eye out for them.
And for the little boat that plies
the water between the ships
and the pilot station near the lighthouse.
I want to see them take a man off the ship
and put another up on board.
I want to spend the day watching this happen
and reach my own conclusions.
I hate to seem greedy — I have so much
to be thankful for already.
But I want to get up early one more morning, at least.
And go to my place with some coffee and wait.
Just wait, to see what's going to happen.

III.
The Knock at the Door

O solitude, my only companion,
muse of marvels, that gave my voice
words I could never ask for!
Answer my question: who am I talking to?

Antonio Machado
from "Dreams in Dialogue"
translated by Dennis Maloney

Juan Ramón Jiménez (1881–1958)

AT FIRST SHE CAME TO ME PURE

At first she came to me pure,
dressed only in her innocence;
and I loved her as we love a child.

Then she began putting on
clothes she picked up somewhere;
and I hated her, without knowing it.

She gradually became a queen,
the jewelry was blinding…
What bitterness and rage!

…She started going back toward nakedness.
And I smiled.

Soon she was back to the single shift
of her old innocence.
I believed in her a second time.

Then she took off the cloth
and was entirely naked…

Naked poetry, always mine,
that I have loved my whole life!

Translated from the Spanish by Robert Bly

Eleanor Wilner (1937–   )

THE MUSE

There she was, for centuries, the big
broad with the luscious tits, the secret
smile, a toga of translucent silk, cool
hand on the shoulder of the suffering
poet—the tease who made him
squeeze those great words out. He
was the mirror *and* the lamp, she the torch
who burned with the blue butane of a pure
refusal, too good for mortal use, her breath
was cold as mountain streams, the chill
of the eternal—no hint of plaque
or any odor of decay. Ethereal as hell,
a spirit in chiffon, the mystery is
how she had got so rounded in the butt
and all her better parts as soft as butter,
why such a wraith should be so ample,
what her endowments had to do
with that for which she set example—
all this was surely Mystery, oh that elusive
object of desire, that 'untouch'd bride
of quietness,' that plump poetic dish
who lived on air but looked
as if she dined on pasta.

Basta!
A pox on the great Lacan
who writes with his eraser, on all poetic
Graces, mute and pensive, concave exactly
where he is most extensive—oh look
what she has *not* that he has got,
a thing I'm too polite to mention
except to say it rhymes with Venus,

72

it was the Latin word for tail;
its root, therefore, is not the same as pen
which comes from the word for feather.

But enough of these fine distinctions.
What a great tradition was born when
Alexander whipped his penknife out, cut
the knot she carefully had tied, leaped
on his mount, a perfect straddle
and let the crotch decide
who was the horse and who was the rider,
who was the muse and who
the writer.

John Berryman (1914–1972)

IMAGES OF ELSPETH

O WHEN I grunted, over lines and her,
my Muse a nymphet & my girl with men
older, of money, continually
lawyers & so, myself a flat-broke Junior.

But the one who made me wild
was who she let take naked photographs
never she showed me but she was proud of.
Unnerving; dire.

My love confused confused with after loves
not ever over time did I outgrow.
Solemn, alone my Muse grew taller.
Rejection slips developed signatures,

many thought Berryman was under weigh,
he wasn't sure himself.
Elspeth became two snapshots in his keeping,
with all her damned clothes on.

She married a Law School dean & flourisheth.
I almost married, with four languages
a ballerina in London, and I should have done.
—Drawing the curtain over fragrant scenes

& interviews malodorous, find me
domestic with my Muse
who had manifested, well, a sense of humour
fatal to bardic pretension.

Dance! from Savannah Garnette with your slur
hypnotic, you'll stay many.

I walked forth to a cold snow to post letters
to a foreign editor & a West Coast critic

wishing I could lay my old hands somewhere on those snapshots.

Meena Alexander (1951–2018)

MUSE

I was young when you came to me.
Each thing rings its turn,
you sang in my ear, a slip of a thing
dressed like a convent girl—
white socks, shoes,
dark blue pinafore, white blouse.

A pencil box in hand: girl, book, tree—
those were the words you gave me.
Girl was *penne,* hair drawn back,
gleaming on the scalp,
the self in a mirror in a rosewood room
the sky at monsoon time, pearl slit.
In cloud cover, a jagged music pours:
gash of sense, raw covenant
clasped still in a gold bound book,
pusthakam pages parted,
ink rubbed with mist,
a bird might have dreamt its shadow there

spreading fire in a tree *maram.*
You murmured the word, sliding it on your tongue,
trying to get how a girl could turn
into a molten thing and not burn.
Centuries later worn out from travel
 I rest under a tree.

You come to me
a bird shedding gold feathers,
each one a quill scraping my tympanum.
You set a book to my ribs.
Night after night I unclasp it at the mirror's edge

alphabets flicker and soar.
Write in the light
of all the languages
you know the earth contains,
you murmur in my ear.
This is pure transport.

Laura Kasischke (1961–)

THE ENORMOUS CAGE

She said, I have a dirty little secret
to tell you. It

will explain everything. And then

she blew it into the beak
of a very tiny bird
in an enormous cage. The

bird, of course, slipped
through the bars and flew away:

What they took with them when they died.
What they almost said but wouldn't say.
Now, one or two on almost
every branch
nearly every sunny day. And

also on the phone lines, even
in the rain. Also, some
nights I feel its miniature

feet tread my spine, then sink in
between my shoulder blades, as if

its dirty little wings were also mine.

Anna Akhmatova (1889–1966)

THE MUSE

When at night I await her coming.
It seems that life hangs by a strand.
What are honors, what is youth, what is freedom,
Compared to that dear guest with rustic pipe in hand.

And she entered. Drawing aside her shawl
She gazed attentively at me.
I said to her: "Was it you who dictated to Dante
The pages of *The Inferno?*" She replied: "It was I."

Translated from the Russian by Judith Hemschemeyer

Carolyn Kizer (1925–2014)

A MUSE OF WATER

We who must act as handmaidens
To our own goddess, turn too fast,
Trip on our hems, to glimpse the muse
Gliding below her lake or sea,
Are left, long-staring after her,
Narcissists by necessity;

Or water-carriers of our young
Till waters burst, and white streams flow
Artesian, from the lifted breast:
Cup-bearers then, to tiny gods,
Imperious table-pounders, who
Are final arbiters of thirst.

Fasten the blouse, and mount the steps
From kitchen taps to Royal Barge,
Assume the trident, don the crown,
Command the Water Music now
That men bestow on Virgin Queens;
Or, goddessing above the waist,

Appear as swan on Thames or Charles
Where iridescent foam conceals
The paddle-stroke beneath the glide:
Immortal feathers preened in poems!
Not our true, intimate nature, stained
By labor, and the casual tide.

Masters of civilization, you
Who moved to river bank from cave,
Putting up tents, and deities,
Though every rivulet wander through

The final, unpolluted glades
To cinder-bank and culvert-lip,

And all the pretty chatterers
Still round the pebbles as they pass
Lightly over their watercourse,
And even the calm rivers flow,
We have, while springs and skies renew,
Dry wells, dead seas, and lingering drouth.

Water itself is not enough.
Harness her turbulence to work
For man: fill his reflecting pools.
Drained for his cofferdams, or stored
In reservoirs for his personal use:
Turn switches! Let the fountains play!

And yet these buccaneers still kneel
Trembling at the water's verge:
"Cool River-Goddess, sweet ravine,
Spirit of pool and shade, inspire!"
So he needs poultice for his flesh.
So he needs water for his fire.

We rose in mists and died in clouds
Or sank below the trammeled soil
To silent conduits underground,
Joining the blind-fish, and the mole.
A gleam of silver in the shale:
Lost murmur! Subterranean moan!

So flows in dark caves, dries away,
What would have brimmed from bank to bank,
Kissing the fields you turned to stone,

81

Under the boughs your axes broke.
And you blame streams for thinning out,
Plundered by man's insatiate want?

Rejoice when a faint music rises
Out of a brackish clump of weeds,
Out of the marsh at ocean-side,
Out of the oil-stained river's gleam,
By the long causeways and gray piers
Your civilizing lusts have made.

Discover the deserted beach
Mere ghosts of curlews safely wade:
Here the warm shallows lave your feet
Like tawny hair of magdalens.
Here, if you care, and lie full-length,
Is water deep enough to drown.

Paul Mariani (1940–   )

FOLLOWING THE LIGHT

In the midst of so much rich uncertain
music he could still get it right for once:
the late late Romantic mirrored in those
giant sea creatures trussed up each day
along the bustling wharf. Eyes glazed
from staring at the naked sun too long,
"clenched beaks coughing for the surge again."

Shelley too in his own brief stay knew
the suicidal drift of swimming toward the light.
As in his lines composed at Lerici,
where fish, drawn by the lamps along
the surface, feel the swack of truth
against their skulls before they are lifted
stunned and gasping into baskets.

Crane watched the phosphorescent swale
of the turtles as they struggled toward
the sundrenched beaches. Hour after hour
he watched, then leapt at last into
the finchurned waters. And when that other
dropped over the sloop's edge, what lamp-
eyed creature was waiting there to greet him?

What is it but a maggot in the brain, the mind
ridden by that whore the Muse? Half bare-
bosomed woman, we say, half conger eel, her song
a drug, her lamp beside her swinging, coaxing
her chosen ones upward toward the light
as we listen to the sounds of words which are
not quite words drifting downward through our element.

Medbh McGuckian (1950–   )

KILLING THE MUSE

My crucified girl,
my Zeus, Satan horns
skin-deep in your oldest cry.
I re-cut your name-to-be
among herbs and lavish gold.

No living woman
was more alive in her sleep, my
least alive of flowers.
Day alone takes your place,
unfinished nightpiece.

It was my first small anguished
crucifixion, the fresh blood drifting
from the last quarry into perfume
spoons, an afterlife
that thinks and knows.

I am shaken, by the storm light
closeness, the closer and closer
wrapping of marble
around your trance-bound body;

I crush my fists
in fringing pleasure
against your lowered eyelids,
their browns that were not shade.

Earth that forced
the fruit to enter
is disappearing
from the landscape.

In your smileless mouth,
a sign of two lips,
a parted male tongue bleeds.
A split-off bone is loosed
from your neck like a pearl necklace.

No one is looking at anyone
if we interlock our fingers,
not to pray,
or your whole body turns to body forth
its underworld of shell-bronze breastplates.

Louise Glück (1943–   )

LUTE SONG

No one wants to be the muse;
in the end, everyone wants to be Orpheus.

Valiantly reconstructed
(out of terror and pain)
and then overwhelmingly beautiful;

restoring, ultimately,
not Eurydice, the lamented one,
but the ardent
spirit of Orpheus, made present

not as a human being, rather
as pure soul rendered
detached, immortal,
through deflected narcissism.

I made a harp of disaster
to perpetuate the beauty of my last love.
Yet my anguish, such as it is,
remains the struggle for form

and my dreams, if I speak openly,
less the wish to be remembered
than the wish to survive,
which is, I believe, the deepest human wish.

IV.
Putting Things Right

The first man who whistled
thought he had a wren in his mouth.
He went around all day
with his lips puckered,
afraid to swallow.

Wendell Berry
"The First"

Jaroslav Seifert (1901–1986)

TO BE A POET

Life taught me long ago
that music and poetry
are the most beautiful things on earth
that life can give us.
Except for love, of course.
In an old textbook
published by the Imperial Printing House
in the year of Vrchlicky's death
I looked up the section on poetics
and poetic ornament.
Then I placed a rose in a tumbler,
lit a candle
and started to write my first verses.
Flare up, flame of words,
and soar,
even if my fingers get burned!
A startling metaphor is worth more
than a ring on one's finger.
But not even Puchmajer's Rhyming Dictionary
was any use to me.
In vain I snatched for ideas
and fiercely closed my eyes
in order to hear that first magic line.
But in the dark, instead of words,
I saw a woman's smile and
wind-blown hair.
That has been my destiny.
And I've been staggering towards it breathlessly
all my life.

Translated from the Czech by Ewald Osers

Carolyn Kizer (1925–2014)

SINGING ALOUD

We all have our faults. Mine is trying to write poems.
New scenery, someone I like, anything sets me off!
I hear my own voice going on, like a god or an oracle,
That cello-tone, intuition. That bell-note of wisdom!

And I can't get rid of the tempting tic of pentameter,
Of the urge to impose a form on what I don't understand,
Or that which I have to transform because it's too grim as it is.
But age is improving me: Now, when I finish a poem

I no longer rush out to impose it on friendly colleagues.
I climb through the park to the reservoir, peer down at my own reflection,
Shake a blossoming branch so I am covered with petals,
Each petal a metaphor...

By the time we reach middle life, we've all been deserted and robbed.
But flowers and grass and animals keep me warm.
And I remind myself to become philosophic:
We are meant to be stripped down, to prepare us for something better,

And, often, I sing aloud. As I grow older
I give way to innocent folly more and more often.
The squirrels and rabbits chime in with inaudible voices.
I feel sure that the birds make an effort to be antiphonal.

When I go to the zoo, the primates and I, in communion,
Hoot at each other, or signal with earthy gestures.
We must move farther out of town, we musical birds and animals,
Or they'll lock us up like the apes, and control us forever.

James Tate (1943–2015)

TEACHING THE APE TO WRITE POEMS

They didn't have much trouble
teaching the ape to write poems:
first they strapped him into the chair,
then tied the pencil around his hand
(the paper had already been nailed down).
Then Dr. Bluespire leaned over his shoulder
and whispered into his ear:
"You look like a god sitting there.
Why don't you try writing something?"

Hu Xudong (1974–)

MAMA ANA PAULA ALSO WRITES POETRY

A tobacco of corn husks in mouth, she throws a thick poetry book
at me, "Read your Mama's poems."
This is true, my student
José's mother,
two Brazils on her chest, a South America on her bucks,
a stomach full of beer, surging like Atlantic,
this Mama Ana Paula
writes poetry. The first day I met her, she lifted me
up like an eagle
catching a small chicken, I wasn't informed She Writes Poetry.
She spat at me her wet words, and rubbed
my face
with her big palm tree fingers. When she licked my
panicked ears
with marijuana tongue, I didn't know She Writes Poetry.
Everyone including her son José and daughter-in-law Gisele said
she was an old Flower Silly, but no one
told me She Writes Poetry.
"Put my teacher down, my dear old Flower Silly." José said.
She dropped me, but went on
vomiting "dick" "dick," and catching "dick"
in the air with her lips. I looked at her
back, strong like hairy bear that kills
a bull even when she's drunk, and I understood:
She Writes Poetry.
But today, when I followed José into the house, and caught a glimpse
of her lying by the pool
with four limbs stretched out, smoking, I didn't think She Writes Poetry
I ran into a ponytail
like Bob Marley, a muscle guy, in the living room, Gisele told me

that's her mother-in-law's guy from last night, I didn't think, even if
you stick me in front of a National Army of China and shoot at my little
torso, that Mama Ana Paula
writes poetry. But Mama Ana Paula
Mama Ana Writes Poetry Paula
writes poetry
which burps and farts. I leafed it through page after page
Mama Ana Paula's poetry book. Yes, Mama Ana Paula writes poetry
indeed. She doesn't write fat poetry, liquor poetry,
marijuana poetry, dick poetry, or muscle poetry of muscle guys.
In a poem called "Three Seconds of Silence in Poetry"
she wrote: "Silence in a poem, give me a minute and in it
I can spin the nine yards of sky."

Translated from the Chinese by Ming Di and Katie Farris

James Lenfestey (1944–   )

STEADY WORK

Steady work, this poetry.
Every night, late, or every morning, early,
with the busy world settled to a forgotten dot or hum.
No sense saving it up, there's always more.
The dark well has no bottom, the dark sky boundless space.
No wages, but no cost. A bit of ink, a scrap of paper,
courage to climb down, wings slowly rising.

Dana Levin (1965–   )

ARS POETICA

Six monarch butterfly cocoons
      clinging to the back of your throat—

      you could feel their gold wings trembling.

You were alarmed. You felt infested.
In the downstairs bathroom of the family home,
      gagging to spit them out—
          and a voice saying, *Don't, don't*—

Zhang Shuguang (1956–   )

TO XUEFEI

Where is your face? flooded by what?
New York streets?
your head, tilted to one side, your neck
can't hold the weight of ideas,
where's your face? you are so clumsy
driving in Brandeis, your wife is
making souvenirs for who? a company?
and your son? in China? Why
you chose this damned
career of a poet,
I can't say...
Your father curses you, your father
I do not know, writes
in a cursive that's yours,
since you are his son and
are in America, and Allen Ginsburg
and John Ashbery
are also there and are beautiful, and you
are hot, but I don't know why
you chose this damned career as a poet.
Wind and your face, poet, is
blurry and strange, I don't understand how these lips
eat steak in a restaurant
if I see you I'll punch you and say Hey Buddy don't lick
your fingers, speak better Chinese, boy,
and I will drag you
from your wife's angry eyes to City Lights,
San Francisco,
City Lights, my Charlie Chaplin. City lights.

Translated from the Chinese by Ming Di and Katie Farris

Lawrence Ferlinghetti (1919–2021)

CONSTANTLY RISKING ABSURDITY…

Constantly risking absurdity
                          and death
whenever he performs
                     above the heads
                               of his audience
the poet like an acrobat
                    climbs on rime
                          to a high wire of his own making
and balancing on eyebeams
                     above a sea of faces
          paces his way
                    to the other side of day
    performing entrechats
                    and sleight-of-foot tricks
and other high theatrics
                     and all without mistaking
          any thing
                    for what it may not be

   For he's the super realist
                     who must perforce perceive
          taut truth
                    before the taking of each stance or step
   in his supposed advance
                     toward that still higher perch
where Beauty stands and waits
                     with gravity
     to start her death-defying leap
And he
     a little charleychaplin man
                     who may or may not catch
     her fair eternal form

spreadeagled in the empty air
of existence

Kimiko Hahn (1955–   )

THE APICULTURALIST
for C

In black veiled hat and canvas gauntlets
Jean Paucton, seventy, climbs the baroque stairs

of the Palais Garnier opera house,
to his rooftop apiary.

The theatrical prop man studied beekeeping
at the Jardin's venerable institute

then hauled onto the seventh-floor ledge
his five weathered crates—

swollen with honey, nearly a thousand pounds a year.

"The bees make an impression, do they not?"
he declares.
                 And you, dear poet?

Your little apiary of simile and syntax—the busy bite
that separates truth from Truth?

Do you not weary of the student manuscript,
that makes elegance
but does nothing to sting cousin or twin? You

who do not flinch in or outside your own sweet studies?
The husband's soft skin? The vial of antidote?
It's a sadistic occupation, is it not?

Louis Simpson (1923–2012)

THE UNWRITTEN POEM

You will never write the poem about Italy.
What Socrates said about love
is true of poetry—where is it?
Not in beautiful faces and distant scenery
but the one who writes and loves.

In your life here, on this street
where the houses from the outside
are all alike, and so are the people.
Inside, the furniture is dreadful—
flock on the walls, and huge color television.

To love and write unrequited
is the poet's fate. Here you'll need
all your ardor and ingenuity.
This is the front and these are the heroes—
a life beginning with "Hi!" and ending with "So long!"

You must rise to the sound of the alarm
and march to catch the 6:20—
watch as they ascend the station platform
and, grasping briefcases, pass beyond your gaze
and hurl themselves into the flames.

Sheryl Luna (1965–   )

LOWERING YOUR STANDARDS FOR FOOD STAMPS

Words fall out of my coat pocket,
soak in bleach water. I touch everyone's
dirty dollars. Maslow's got everything on me.
Fourteen hours on my feet. No breaks.
No smokes or lunch. Blank-eyed movements:
trash bags, coffee burner, fingers numb.
I am hourly protestations and false smiles.
The clock clicks its slow slowing.
Faces blur in a stream of hurried soccer games,
sunlight, and church certainty. I have no
poem to carry, no material illusions.
Cola spilled on hands, so sticky fingered,
I'm far from poems. I'd write of politicians,
refineries, and a border's barbed wire,
but I am unlearning America's languages
with a mop. In a summer-hot red
polyester top, I sell lotto tickets. Cars wait for gas
billowing black. Killing time has new meaning.
A jackhammer breaks apart a life. The slow globe
spirals, and at night black space has me dizzy.
Visionaries off their meds and wacked out
meth heads sing to me. A panicky fear of robbery
and humiliation drips with my sweat.
Words some say are weeping twilight and sunrise.
I am drawn to dramas, the couple arguing, the man
headbutting his wife in the parking lot.
911: no metered aubade, and nobody but
myself to blame.

Wallace Stevens (1879–1955)

THE MAN ON THE DUMP

Day creeps down. The moon is creeping up.
The sun is a corbeil of flowers the moon Blanche
Places there, a bouquet. Ho-ho...The dump is full
Of images. Days pass like papers from a press.
The bouquets come here in the papers. So the sun,
And so the moon, both come, and the janitor's poems
Of every day, the wrapper on the can of pears,
The cat in the paper-bag, the corset, the box
From Esthonia: the tiger chest, for tea.

The freshness of night has been fresh a long time.
The freshness of morning, the blowing of day, one says
That it puffs as Cornelius Nepos reads, it puffs
More than, less than or it puffs like this or that.
The green smacks in the eye, the dew in the green
Smacks like fresh water in a can; like the sea
On a cocoanut—how many men have copied dew
For buttons, how many women have covered themselves
With dew, dew dresses, stories and chains of dew, heads
Of the floweriest flowers dewed with the dewiest dew.
One grows to hate these things except on the dump.

Now, in the time of spring (azaleas, trilliums,
Myrtle, viburnums, daffodils, blue phlox),
Between that disgust and this, between the things
That are on the dump (azaleas and so on)
And those that will be (azaleas and so on),
One feels the purifying change. One rejects
The trash.

That's the moment when the moon creeps up
To the bubbling of bassoons. That's the time
One looks at the elephant-colorings of tires.
Everything is shed; and the moon comes up as the moon
(All its images are in the dump) and you see
As a man (not like an image of a man),
You see the moon rise in the empty sky.

One sits and beats an old tin can, lard pail.
One beats and beats for that which one believes.
That's what one wants—to get near. Could it after all
Be merely oneself, as superior as the ear
To a crow's voice? Did the nightingale torture the ear,
Pack the heart and scratch the mind? And does the ear
Solace itself in peevish birds? Is it peace,
Is it a philosopher's honeymoon, one finds
On the dump? Is it to sit among mattresses of the dead,
Bottles, pots, shoes and grass and murmur *aptest eve:*
Is it to hear the blatter of grackles and say
Invisible priest; is it to eject, to pull
The day to pieces and cry *stanza my stone?*
Where was it one first heard of the truth? The the.

Elizabeth Spires (1952–   )

THE WOMAN ON THE DUMP

> *Where was it one first heard of the truth? The the.*
> —Wallace Stevens

She sits on a smoldering couch
reading labels from old tin cans,
the ground ground down
to dirt, hard as poured cement.
A crowd of fat white gulls
take mincing, oblique steps
around the couch, searching for
an orange rind, a crab claw.
Clouds scud backward overhead,
drop quickly over the horizon,
as if weighted with lead sinkers.
The inside's outside here,
her "sitting room" *en plein air:*
a homey triad of chaise longue,
tilting table, and old floor lamp
from a torn-down whorehouse,
the shade a painted scene
of nymphs in a naked landscape.
The lamp is a beautiful thing,
even if she can't plug it in,
the bare-cheeked, breathless
nymphs part of the eternal
feminine as they rush away
from streaming trees and clouds
that can't be trusted not to change
from man to myth and back again.

The dump's too real. Or not
real enough. It is hot here.
Or cold. When the sun goes down,
she wraps herself in old newspaper,
the newsprint rubbing off,
so that she is the news as she
looks for clues and scraps
of things in the refuse. The *the*
is here somewhere, buried
under bulldozed piles of trash.
She picks up a pair of old cymbals
to announce the moon, the pure
symbol, just coming up over there.
Abandoned bathtubs, sinks, and stoves
glow white—abstract forms
in the moonlight—a high tide
of garbage spawns and grows,
throwing long lovely shadows
across unplumbed ravines and gullies.
She'll work through the night,
the woman on the dump,
sifting and sorting and putting
things right, saving everything
that can be saved, rejecting
nothing, piles of tires
in the background unexhaustedly
burning, burning, burning.

Pablo Neruda (1904–1973)

ARS POETICA (1)

As a poet-carpenter
I first seek the wood
rough or smooth, so inclined
with my hands I touch the scent,
I smell the color, pass my fingers
over the fragrant integrity,
through the silence of the system,
until I sleep or pass to another body,
or take off my clothes or submerge myself
in the health of the wood,
in its round ramparts.

The second thing I do is cut
with the sizzling saw
the table recently selected:
from the table rise the verses
like liberated splinters,
fragrant, strong and distant,
and so now, my poem,
have a deck, a hull, careening,
arise beside the road,
be inhabited by the sea.

As a poet-baker
I prepare the fire, the flour,
the leavening, the heart,
and I, involved up to the elbows,
kneading the light of the oven,
the green water of language,
so the bread that happens to me
sells itself in the bakery.

I am, and know not whether they know it,
a blacksmith by destiny
or at least I sponsored
for everyone and for myself
metallurgical poetry.

With such open patronage
I did not forge ardent bonds:
I was a solitary ironmonger.
Seeking broken horseshoes
I flowed with my slag
to a region without inhabitants,
illuminated by the wind.
There I found new metals
that I converted into words.

I understand that my experiences
as a metaphysician of hands
may not serve poetry,
but I grew out my claws
attacking my works,
and those are the poor recipes
I learned with my own hands:
if they are proved useless
in the practice of poetry,
I immediately relent:
I smile for the future
and retire in advance.

Translated from the Spanish by William O'Daly

Cornelius Eady (1954–)

DANCE AT THE AMHERST COUNTY PUBLIC LIBRARY

Fellow poets,
My Brothers and Sisters,
Comrades,
Distinguished guests and visitors,
Yes,
Even the tourists
In their T-shirts and mirrored sunglasses.

Before our attention begins to wander
Let me ask this:
In one hundred years,
No,
Say fifty years,
If, through grand design or fluke
The world still stands
And leads our descendants to this branch library in Amherst, Va.

Which poets would they find on the shelves?

The answer probably is
They will only find
What I found this afternoon:
Shakespeare
And Paul Laurence Dunbar.

In view of
And in spite of this awful truth
I would still like to leave one or two thoughts behind:
If you are an archaeologist and find these items slipped into
        Mr. Dunbar's *Collected Works:*

This poem,
A pair of red laces

Please understand that this was how I defined myself,
A dancing fool who couldn't stay away from words
Even though they brought me nothing but difficulties.
I was better when I danced,
The language of the body so much cleaner.

I was always in jealous awe of the dancers,
Who seemed, to me at least, to be honest animals.
When I danced

I imagined myself a woman,
Because there is no sight more lovely
Than a woman kicking her heels up in a dive.

This is how I wasted my time,
Trying to become the Henry Ford of poetry,
And mass produce a group of words
Into a thing that could shake
And be owned by the entire world.

Naturally, I failed.

Of course, even the failure was a sort of dance.

My friend,
I bequeath to you what I know:
Not the image of a high, glistening city
But the potential in tall grass, flattened
by a summer's storm.
Not the dance
But the good intentions of a dance.

This was the world I belonged to,
With its symphony of near-misses,
And in its name
And in the names of all those omitted
I dance my small graffiti dance.

Ellen Bryant Voigt (1943–)

DANCING WITH POETS

"The accident" is what he calls the time
he threw himself from a window four floors up,
breaking his back and both ankles, so that walking
became the direst labor for this man
who takes my hand, invites me to the empty strip of floor
that fronts the instruments, a length of polished wood
the shape of a grave. *Unsuited for this world—*
his body bears the marks of it, his hand
is tense with effort and with shame, and I shy away
from any audience, but I love to dance, and soon
we find a way to move, drifting apart as each
effects a different ripple across the floor,
a plaid and a stripe to match the solid navy of the band.
And suddenly the band is getting better, so pleased
to have this pair of dancers, since we make evident
the music in the noise—and the dull pulse
leaps with unexpected riffs and turns, we can hear
how good the keyboard really is, the bright cresting
of another major key as others join us: a strict
block of a man, a formidable cliff of mind, dancing
as if melted, as if unhinged; his partner a gift of brave
elegance to those who watch her dance; and at her elbow,
Berryman back from the bridge, and Frost, relieved
of grievances, Dickinson waltzing there with lavish Keats,
who coughs into a borrowed handkerchief—all the poets of exile
and despair, unfit for this life, all those who cannot speak
but only sing, all those who cannot walk
who strut and spin until the waiting citizens at the bar,
aloof, judgmental, begin to sway or drum their straws
or hum, leave their seats to crowd the narrow floor
and now we are one body, swearing and foolish,
one body with its clear pathetic grace, not

lifted out of grief but dancing it, transforming
for one night this local bar, before we're turned back out
to our separate selves, to the dangerous streets and houses,
to the overwhelming drone of the living world.

Patricia Hampl (1946–)

MOTHER-DAUGHTER DANCE

Because it is late
because we fought today
because it was hot
and heat is an excuse
to be alone,
I sit in this chair stuffed
with old sun, leftover heat.

Our fight. The subject as always was history.
You made me look over my shoulder.
Mother was back there, speaking
to us in epilepsy, that language
she learned on her own,
the one we encouraged her to use
at the dinner table.
In my mind, I fell down, writhing,
trying to make history repeat itself,
burning with translations of guilt
for the men in the family.
Father forced a yellow pencil
between Mother's teeth, like a rose:
you die if you swallow your tongue.

All afternoon you yelled at me
as I slithered nearer to her.
We were doing the mother-daughter sweat dance,
salt dance, sexy Spanish rose dance.
You were yelling from the English language,
that fringed island I swim toward at night.
"The pencil," you were screaming in your language,
"Take the pencil from her mouth.
Write it down,
write your message down."

Sharon Olds (1942–   )

I GO BACK TO MAY 1937

I see them standing at the formal gates of their colleges,
I see my father strolling out
under the ochre sandstone arch, the
red tiles glinting like bent
plates of blood behind his head, I
see my mother with a few light books at her hip
standing at the pillar made of tiny bricks,
the wrought-iron gate still open behind her, its
sword-tips aglow in the May air,
they are about to graduate, they are about to get married,
they are kids, they are dumb, all they know is they are
innocent, they would never hurt anybody.
I want to go up to them and say Stop,
don't do it—she's the wrong woman,
he's the wrong man, you are going to do things
you cannot imagine you would ever do,
you are going to do bad things to children,
you are going to suffer in ways you have not heard of,
you are going to want to die. I want to go
up to them there in the late May sunlight and say it,
her hungry pretty face turning to me,
her pitiful beautiful untouched body,
his arrogant handsome face turning to me,
his pitiful beautiful untouched body,
but I don't do it. I want to live. I
take them up like the male and female
paper dolls and bang them together
at the hips, like chips of flint, as if to
strike sparks from them, I say
Do what you are going to do, and I will tell about it.

Lisel Mueller (1924–2020)

WHEN I AM ASKED

When I am asked
how I began writing poems,
I talk about the indifference of nature.

It was soon after my mother died,
a brilliant June day,
everything blooming.

I sat on a gray stone bench
in a lovingly planted garden,
but the daylilies were as deaf
as the ears of drunken sleepers
and the roses curved inward.
Nothing was black or broken
and not a leaf fell
and the sun blared endless commercials
for summer holidays.

I sat on a gray stone bench
ringed with the ingenue faces
of pink and white impatiens
and placed my grief
in the mouth of language,
the only thing that would grieve with me.

Tess Gallagher (1943–)

I STOP WRITING THE POEM

to fold the clothes. No matter who lives
or who dies, I'm still a woman.
I'll always have plenty to do.
I bring the arms of his shirt
together. Nothing can stop
our tenderness. I'll get back
to the poem. I'll get back to being
a woman. But for now
there's a shirt, a giant shirt
in my hands, and somewhere a small girl
standing next to her mother
watching to see how it's done.

Ed Bok Lee (n. d.)

WOKE

I was wrestling with a poem
while in a far room she was crying.
I'd been sweating to get it to sing
or sputter sense; at least exorcize
the animus from our deeply lodged insanity.

Meanwhile, in her far room, Babygirl would not go back down.

I needed personally to hear through the poem
what future humans will believe over the next few millennia
of horror, tenderness, genocide, altruism, capacity for deceit, of beauty—

I didn't understand she was freely translating,
while the poem I hunched over lay comatose.

Our policy: wait five to ten minutes before going in.
Often, after a final, hawk-like screech, she'd fall quiet, and I could breathe.
But on this night, the longer she wailed, the more deaths shed from me,
until finally at the risk of waking her forever
I rose and wandered into the dark corner of our galaxy
where a deeper belief in the brightness of human souls
was now livid in its demand for a billion new tragio-comedies.

Marilyn Nelson (1946–   )

BALI HAI CALLS MAMA

As I was putting away the groceries
I'd spent the morning buying
for the week's meals I'd planned
around things the baby could eat,
things my husband would eat,
and things I should eat
because they aren't too fattening,
late on a Saturday afternoon
after flinging my coat on a chair
and wiping the baby's nose
while asking my husband
what he'd fed it for lunch
and whether
the medicine I'd brought for him
had made his cough improve,
wiping the baby's nose again,
checking its diaper,
stepping over the baby
who was reeling to and from
the bottom kitchen drawer
with pots, pans, and plastic cups,
occasionally clutching the hem of my skirt
and whining to be held,
I was half listening for the phone
which never rings for me
to ring for me
and someone's voice to say that
I could forget about handing back
my students' exams which I'd had for a week,
that I was right about *The Waste Land*,
that I'd been given a raise,

118

all the time wondering
how my sister was doing,
whatever happened to my old lover(s),
and why my husband wanted
a certain brand of toilet paper;
and I wished I hadn't, but I'd bought
another fashion magazine that promised
to make me beautiful by Christmas,
and there wasn't room for the creamed corn
and every time I opened the refrigerator door
the baby rushed to grab whatever was on the bottom shelf
which meant I constantly had to wrestle
jars of its mushy food out of its sticky hands
and I stepped on the baby's hand and the baby was screaming
and I dropped the bag of cake flour I'd bought to make cookies with
and my husband rushed in to find out what was wrong because the baby
was drowning out the sound of the touchdown although I had scooped
it up and was holding it in my arms so its crying was inside
my head like an echo in a barrel and I was running cold water
on its hand while somewhere in the back of my mind wondering what
to say about *The Waste Land* and whether I could get away with putting
        broccoli in a meatloaf when

suddenly through the window
came the wild cry of geese.

V.
All This Fiddle

We turn and turn in the animal belly,
in the mineral belly, in the belly of time.
To find the way out: the poem.

Octavio Paz
from "Toward the Poem"
translated by Eliot Weinberger

Marianne Moore (1887–1972)

POETRY

I, too, dislike it: there are things that are important beyond all this fiddle.
Reading it, however, with a perfect contempt for it, one discovers in
it after all, a place for the genuine.
Hands that can grasp, eyes
that can dilate, hair that can rise
if it must, these things are important not because a
high-sounding interpretation can be put upon them but because they are
useful. When they become so derivative as to become unintelligible,
the same thing may be said for all of us, that we
do not admire what
we cannot understand: the bat
holding on upside down or in quest of something to
eat, elephants pushing, a wild horse taking a roll, a tireless wolf under
a tree, the immovable critic twinkling his skin like a horse that feels a flea,
        the baseball fan, the statistician—
nor is it valid
to discriminate against 'business documents and school-books';
all these phenomena are important. One must make a distinction
however: when dragged into prominence by half poets, the result is not poetry,
nor till the poets among us can be
'literalists of the imagination-' above
insolence and triviality and can present
for inspection, 'imaginary gardens with real toads in them,' shall we have
it. In the meantime, if you demand on one hand,
the raw material of poetry in
all its rawness, and
that which is on the other hand
genuine, then you are interested in poetry.

Wislawa Szymborska (1923–2012)

SOME PEOPLE LIKE POETRY

Some people—
that means not everyone.
Not even most of them, only a few.
Not counting school, where you have to,
and poets themselves,
you might end up with something like two per thousand.

Like—
but then, you can like chicken soup,
or compliments, or the color blue,
your old scarf,
your own way,
petting the dog.

Poetry—
but what is poetry anyway?
More than one rickety answer
has tumbled since that question first was raised.
But I just keep on not knowing, and I cling to that
like a redemptive handrail.

Translated from the Polish by Clare Cavanagh and Stanislaw Baranczak

Dean Young (1955–   )

SINGING UNDERWATER

What is poetry anyway? My dream
or yours or amalgam of everyone's?
Oneiric eyeball in a tree's bark
or ordinary gulp of air? The hark,
hark of an afterlife or face-plant
in the mud? No matter how many versions
I read, it ends the same: daisies
on a pile of sand while they're burning
the furniture, scraping the walls,
smashing the crockery as dictated by law.
Do you think nightingales even know
if they're being heard? Divine intervention?
Give me a break. Things happen wrong
all the time: the song is singed, burnt
is fired, the lightbulb goes on in the ghost
story. Some days it's hard to withstand
all the demystification, every angel
an angel of demystification despite
her secret cookie recipe. Is it all
just churched-up box mix, moondust
quackery? Doubtlessly confusion
must be banished although some beguiling
hiss of vagaries should remain to catalyze
the confinement of wonderment glowing
in the test tube somehow cool to the touch,
such brevities that evoke eternity.
Scarecrow with a migraine? Gate unhinged?
Words vanishing as whims but staining
the rib cage I mean page. Thus poetry's
most often ambiguous, conciliatory maybes,
no musts but mists, something between

the strict rules of dominoes and a mind's
high disquiet, a few thank-you notes
written in blood.

James Scully (1937–   )

WHAT IS POETRY

We know it doesn't rhyme much anymore
but is it beautiful is it true
does it transcend the moment
which moment

or is it ironic, does it echo, echo what
does it have ears

at night whom does it adore
yet at dawn
what dream would it go to the wall for

or is it vituperative, why not
doesn't it express powerful, feeling,
an overflow of feeling, is it sincere
is that enough

does it lay bare the soul
or explore the give-and-take of intense personal
     interrelationships
which persons, what kinds of interrelationships
work or play or
why one and not the others

is it witty, profound, wittily profound, profoundly witty,
is it avant-garde does it shock the bourgeoisie
who love it

or is it above the social arena does it circle the earth,
     a satellite with a proper sense of gravity high
     above the winds of fashion
who put it up there
does it transmit breathtaking pictures of a tiny earth

is it a world created by the poet
for the poet of the poet
does it exist for its own sake,
but if it's a way of breathing, whose way
do they smoke are they
breathing making love or getting off work

is it the ideology of a class or the puff of genius
genius for what what class
what are you talking about
is it a man speaking to men
a woman speaking to women
or universal human speaking
to no one in particular
that is, no one at all

is it a mirror held up to nature,
to human nature,
or is it an escape, is it
a mirror held up to nature, to escape human nature, or
a mirror held up to human nature
to escape human history

are you afraid of it
do you understand it

does it embody human values,
values as they are
or as they say they are,
which humans, which values
is it for or against
or does it take no position,

where did it go then
does it levitate, is it in heaven

is it then beyond all this
what is it, where, if you know tell us

but if you don't know
shut up, we'll understand

Elizabeth Alexander (1962–   )

ARS POETICA #100: I BELIEVE

Poetry, I tell my students,
is idiosyncratic. Poetry

is where we are ourselves
(though Sterling Brown said

"Every 'I' is a dramatic 'I'"),
digging in the clam flats

for the shell that snaps,
emptying the proverbial pocketbook.

Poetry is what you find
in the dirt in the corner,

overhear on the bus, God
in the details, the only way

to get from here to there.
Poetry (and now my voice is rising)

is not all love, love, love,   ·
and I'm sorry the dog died.

Poetry (here I hear myself loudest)
is the human voice,

and are we not of interest to each other?

B. H. Fairchild (1942–   )

WHAT HE SAID

When Candi Baumeister announced to us all
that J.D. was *in love* with Brigitte Bardot,
drawing those two syllables out like some kid
stretching pink strands of Dubble Bubble
from between her teeth, J.D. chose not
to duck his head in the unjust shame
of the truly innocent but rather lifted it
in the way of his father scanning the sky
in silent prayer for the grace of rain abundant
upon his doomed soybeans or St. Francis
blessing sparrows or the air itself, eyes radiant
with Truth and Jesus, and said, *Babydoll,*
I would walk on my tongue from here to Amarillo
just to wash her dishes.
                              There is a time
in the long affliction of our spoken lives when,
among all the verbal bungling, stupidity,
and general disorder that burden us
like the ragged garment of the flesh itself, when,
beneath the vast and articulate shadows
of the saints of language, the white dove of genius
with its quick, wild wings has entered our souls,
our immaculate ignorance, and we are,
at last, redeemed. And so is conceived and born
the thing said, finally, *well*—nay, *perfectly*—
as it might be said by that unknowable Being
for whom we have in our mortal linguistic
incapacity no adequate name except the one
Candi Baumeister bore in her own virginal moment
of absolute poetry: *My God, J.D.*

131

Czeslaw Milosz (1911–2004)

ARS POETICA?

I have always aspired to a more spacious form
that would be free from the claims of poetry or prose
and would let us understand each other without exposing
the author or reader to subline agonies.

In the very essence of poetry there is something indecent:
a thing is brought forth which we didn't know we had in us,
so we blink our eyes, as if a tiger had sprung out
and stood in the light, lashing his tail.

That's why poetry is rightly said to be dictated by a daimonion,
though it's an exaggeration to maintain that he must be an angel.
It's hard to guess where that pride of poets comes from,
when so often they're put to shame by the disclosure of their frailty.

What reasonable man would like to be a city of demons,
who behave as if they were at home, speak in many tongues,
and who, not satisfied with stealing his lips or hand,
work at changing his destiny for their convenience?

It's true that what is morbid is highly valued today,
and so you may think that I am only joking
or that I've devised just one more means
of praising Art with the help of irony.

There was a time when only wise books were read,
helping us to bear our pain and misery.
This, after all, is not quite the same
as leafing through a thousand works fresh from psychiatric clinics.

And yet the world is different from what it seems to be
and we are other than how we see ourselves in our ravings.
People therefore preserve silent integrity,
thus earning the respect of their relatives and neighbors.

The purpose of poetry is to remind us
how difficult it is to remain just one person,
for our house is open, there are no keys in the doors,
and invisible guests come in and out at will.

What I'm saying here is not, I agree, poetry,
as poems should be written rarely and reluctantly,
under unbearable duress and only with the hope
that good spirits, not evil ones, choose us for their instrument.

Translated from the Polish by Czeslaw Milosz and Lillian Vallee

Eleanor Wilner (1937–   )

ARS POETICA

They wanted from us
loud despairs, ear-
splitting syntactical tricks, our guts
hung up to the light, privacy
dusted off and displayed, in ways
elliptical and clever, or
in a froth of spleen—details
of the damages, musings on divorce,
ashtrays from motels: films shot
on location, life made almost real
by its private dislocations. This
they said, was the true
grit, the way it is, no lies, the heart
laid open as a pancake griddle to the awful
heat of rage, rage and desire, coiled beneath
and glowing, until even a drop of sweat
or ink, let fall in its vicinity,
would sizzle. And over all, the big I
swollen like a jellyfish, quivering
and venomous. These things were
our imperative: the poet
in his stained T-shirt, all gripes
and belly, and, well, so *personable*—
my god, so like ourselves!
Oh yes, the women poets, too, so
unashamed, ripping off their masks
like nylon stockings.

***

And all the time, the shy and shapely
mind, like some Eurydice, wanders—

darkened by veils, a shade
with measured footsteps. So many things are gone
and the end of the world looms
like a shark's fin on the flats of our horizon.
Fatigue sets in, and the wind rises.
The door is swinging on its hinges—the room
pried open, the one upstairs in Bluebeard's castle.
They have been hanging there a long time
in their bridal dresses, from hooks,
by their own long hair.
The wind that makes them sway until
they seem almost alive
is like the rush of our compassion.
Yes, now we remember them all
and the sea with its unchanging heaving—a grief
as deep and as dactylic as the voice of Homer,
and, as we turn another way, we lay the past out
on Achilles' shield, abandon it to earth,
our common ground—the bridal hope, its murder,
the old, old story, perpetual
as caring: the scant human store
that is so strangely self-restoring
and whose sufficiency
is our continual surprise.

Tracy K. Smith (1972–   )

AN OLD STORY

We were made to understand it would be
Terrible. Every small want, every niggling urge,
Every hate swollen to a kind of epic wind.

Livid, the land, and ravaged, like a rageful
Dream. The worst in us having taken over
And broken the rest utterly down.

                        A long age
Passed. When at last we knew how little
Would survive us—how little we had mended

Or built that was not now lost—something
Large and old awoke. And then our singing
Brought on a different manner of weather.

Then animals long believed gone crept down
From trees. We took new stock of one another.
We wept to be reminded of such color.

Layli Long Soldier (n. d.)

from VAPORATIVE

When I want to write seriously I think of people like
dg for whom I wrote a long poem for whom I revised
until the poem forgot its way back troubled I let it go when
you love something let it go if it returns be a good mother
father welcome the poem open armed pull out the frying
pan grease it coat it prepare a meal
apron and kitchen sweat labor
my love my sleeves pushed
to elbows like the old days a sack
of flour and keys I push them
typography and hotcakes work
seduce a poem into believing
I can home it I can provide it
white gravy whatever the craving
poem eat and lie down full
poem rest here full don't
lift a single I
etter.

Larry Levis (1946–1996)

THE POEM YOU ASKED FOR

My poem would eat nothing.
I tried giving it water
but it said no,

worrying me.
Day after day,
I held it up to the light,

turning it over,
but it only pressed its lips
more tightly together.

It grew sullen, like a toad
through with being teased.
I offered it all my money,

my clothes, my car with a full tank.
But the poem stared at the floor.
Finally I cupped it in

my hands, and carried it gently
out into the soft air, into the
evening traffic, wondering how

to end things between us.
For now it had begun breathing,
putting on more and

more hard rings of flesh.
And the poem demanded the food,
it drank up all the water,

beat me and took my money,
tore the faded clothes
off my back,

said Shit,
and walked slowly away,
slicking its hair down.

Said it was going
over to your place.

Tomas Tranströmer (1931–2015)

MORNING BIRD SONGS

I wake up my car;
pollen covers the windshield.
I put my dark glasses on.
The bird songs all turn dark.

Meanwhile someone is buying a paper
at the railroad station
not far from a big freight car
reddened all over with rust.
It shimmers in the sun.

The whole universe is full.

A cool corridor cuts through the spring warmth;
a man comes hurrying past
describing how someone right up in the main office
has been telling lies about him.

Through a backdoor in the landscape
the magpie arrives,
black and white, bird of the death-goddess.
A blackbird flies back and forth
until the whole scene becomes a charcoal drawing,
except for the white clothes on the line:
a Palestrina choir.

The whole universe is full!

Fantastic to feel how my poem is growing
while I myself am shrinking.

It's getting bigger, it's taking my place,
it's pressing against me.
It has shoved me out of the nest.
The poem is finished.

Translated from the Swedish by Robert Bly

George Oppen (1908–1984)

THE POEM

how shall I light
this room that measures years

and years not miracles nor were we
judged but a direction

of things in us burning burning for we are not
still nor is this place a wind
utterly outside ourselves and yet it is
unknown and all the sails full to the last

rag of the topgallant, royal
tops'l, the least rags
at the mast-heads

to save the commonplace save myself Tyger
Tyger still burning in me burning
in the night sky burning
in us the light

in the room it was all
part of the wars
of things brilliance
of things

in the appalling
seas language

lives and wakes us together
out of sleep the poem
opens its dazzling whispering hands

Stephen Dobyns (1941–   )

PASSING THE WORD

The poem as object; communicable; naked
as a mannequin after closing, stripped
between dressings, wig torn off, arms and legs
piled on the floor—the ability to rebuild,
a movement from nothing. The poem as bell
and the mannequin's head as clapper: a silent bell,
insistently proclaiming. Dogs stir. A cat
moves into shadow: now a jungle, now a tiger.
The poem at your front door at three in the morning,
leaning on a bell echoing in both of you,
which becomes both of you, coming together
from different directions. And caught by the sound,
you stumble downstairs; a single slipper and slap
of a bare foot; tugging at your robe; finding
the light which doesn't work. You open the door
and there is the mannequin dressed in dark silks—
a jumble of arms and legs for you to assemble;
its face white except for the mouth, a red river
between the ears; and the eyes which are empty.
And you would say something, searching for anger
beneath stones, some counterblow, some final
definition. But you wait too long and now your face,
at best never more than tacked on, begins to slide,
drip like a bad tap between your slipper
and one bare foot. And you would move your arms,
legs, but suddenly they are moving into you,
into your body like sleeves turned inside out.
You are unnecessarily afraid. There is no harm here.
You can refuse to accept it and in the morning
it will be gone and you will have forgotten it,
rearranged your face with a nail in the forehead.
You will leave your front steps as it will have left

the house you have opened to it and your wife with
her half smile and dreams of trees heavy with apples.

Archibald MacLeish (1892–1982)

ARS POETICA

A poem should be palpable and mute
As a globed fruit,

Dumb
As old medallions to the thumb,

Silent as the sleeve-worn stone
Of casement ledges where the moss has grown—

A poem should be wordless
As the flight of birds.

*

A poem should be motionless in time
As the moon climbs,

Leaving, as the moon releases
Twig by twig the night-entangled trees,

Leaving, as the moon behind the winter leaves,
Memory by memory the mind—

A poem should be motionless in time
As the moon climbs.

*

A poem should be equal to:
Not true.

For all the history of grief
An empty doorway and a maple leaf.

For love
The leaning grasses and two lights above the sea—

A poem should not mean
But be.

Terrance Hayes (1971–   )

ARS POETICS WITH BACON

Fortunately, the family, anxious about its diminishing
food supply, encountered a small, possibly hostile pig
along the way. The daughter happened upon it first
pushing its scuffed snout against something hidden
at the base of a thornbush: a blood-covered egg, maybe,
or small rubber ball exactly like the sort that snapped
from the paddle my mother used to beat me with
when I let her down. At the time the father and mother
were tangled in some immemorial dispute about cause
and effect: who'd harmed whom first, how jealousy
did not, in fact, begin as jealousy but as desperation.
When the daughter called out to them, they turned
to see her lift the pig, it was no heavier than an orphan,
from the bushes and then set it down in their path.
They waited to see whether the pig might idle forward
with them until they made camp or wander back toward
the home they'd abandoned to war. Night, enclosed
in small drops of rain, began to fall upon them.
"Consequence" is the word that splintered my mind.
Walking a path in the dark is about something
the way a family is about something. Like the pig,
I too, wanted to reach through the thorns for the egg
or ball believing, it was a symbol of things to come.
I wanted to roll it in my palm like the head
of a small redbird until it sang to me. I wanted
to know how my mother passed her days having
never touched her husband's asshole, for example.
Which parts of your body have never been touched,
I wanted to ask. I'd been hired to lead the family
from danger to a territory full of more seeds than bullets,
but, truth was, in the darkness there was no telling
what was rooting in the soil. Plots of complete silence,

romantics posing in a field bludgeoned by shame.
The heart, biologically speaking, is ugly as it pumps
its passion and fear down the veins. Which is to say,
starting out we have no wounds to speak of
beyond the ways our parents expressed their love.
We were never sure what the pig was after or whether
it was, in fact, not a pig but some single-minded soul
despair turned into a pig, some devil worthy of mercy.
Without giving away the enigmatic ending, I will say,
when we swallowed the flesh, our eyes were closed.

Galway Kinnell (1927–2014)

THE BEAR

1

In late winter
I sometimes glimpse bits of steam
coming up from
some fault in the old snow
and bend close and see it is lung-colored
and put down my nose
and know
the chilly, enduring odor of bear.

2

I take a wolf's rib and whittle
it sharp at both ends
and coil it up
and freeze it in blubber and place it out
on the fairway of the bears.

And when it has vanished
I move out on the bear tracks,
roaming in circles
until I come to the first, tentative, dark
splash on the earth.

And I set out
running, following the splashes
of blood wandering over the world.
At the cut, gashed resting places
I stop and rest,
at the crawl-marks
where he lay out on his belly
to overpass some stretch of bauchy ice
I lie out

dragging myself forward with bear-knives in my fists.

     3
On the third day I begin to starve,
at nightfall I bend down as I knew I would
at a turd sopped in blood,
and hesitate, and pick it up,
and thrust it in my mouth, and gnash it down,
and rise
and go on running.

     4
On the seventh day,
living by now on bear blood alone,
I can see his upturned carcass far out ahead, a scraggled,
steamy hulk,
the heavy fur riffling in the wind.

I come up to him
and stare at the narrow-spaced, petty eyes,
the dismayed
face laid back on the shoulder, the nostrils
flared, catching
perhaps the first taint of me as he
died.

I hack
a ravine in his thigh, and eat and drink,
and tear him down his whole length
and open him and climb in
and close him up after me, against the wind,
and sleep.

5

And dream
of lumbering flatfooted
over the tundra,
stabbed twice from within,
splattering a trail behind me,
splattering it out no matter which way I lurch,

no matter which parabola of bear-transcendence,
which dance of solitude I attempt,
which gravity-clutched leap,
which trudge, which groan.

6

Until one day I totter and fall—
fall on this
stomach that has tried so hard to keep up,
to digest the blood as it leaked in,
to break up
and digest the bone itself: and now the breeze
blows over me, blows off
the hideous belches of ill-digested bear blood
and rotted stomach
and the ordinary, wretched odor of bear,

blows across
my sore, lolled tongue a song
or screech, until I think I must rise up
and dance. And I lie still.

7

I awaken I think. Marshlights
reappear, geese
come trailing again up the flyway.

In her ravine under old snow the dam-bear
lies, licking
lumps of smeared fur
and drizzly eyes into shapes
with her tongue. And one
hairy-soled trudge stuck out before me,
the next groaned out,
the next,
the next,
the rest of my days I spend
wandering: wondering
what, anyway,
was that sticky infusion,
that rank flavor of blood,
that poetry, by which I lived?

VI.
The Real Work

Tell all the Truth but tell it slant—
Success in Circuit lies
Too bright for our infirm Delight
The Truth's superb surprise
As Lightning to the Children eased
With explanation kind
The Truth must dazzle gradually
Or every man be blind—

Emily Dickinson
"Tell All the Truth but Tell It Slant"

Jacques Prevert (1900–1977)

TO PAINT THE PORTRAIT OF A BIRD

First paint a cage
with an open door
then paint
something pretty
something simple
something beautiful
something useful
for the bird
then place the canvas against a tree
in a garden
in a wood
or in a forest
hide behind the tree
without speaking
without moving...
Sometimes the bird comes quickly
but he can just as well spend long years
before deciding
Don't get discouraged
wait
wait years if necessary
the swiftness or slowness of the coming
of the bird having no rapport
with the success of the picture
When the bird comes
if he comes
observe the most profound silence
wait till the bird enters the cage
and when he has entered

gently close the door with a brush
then
paint out all the bars one by one
taking care not to touch any of the feathers of the bird
Then paint the portrait of the tree
choosing the most beautiful of its branches
for the bird
paint also the green foliage and the wind's freshness
the dust of the sun
and the noise of insects in the summer heat
and then wait for the bird to decide to sing
If the bird doesn't sing
it's a bad sign
a sign that the painting is bad
but if he sings it's a good sign
a sign that you can sign
so then so gently you pull out one
of the feathers of the bird
and you write your name in a corner of the picture

Translated from the French by Lawrence Ferlinghetti

William Carlos Williams (1883–1963)

TRACT

I will teach you my townspeople
how to perform a funeral
for you have it over a troop
of artists—
unless one should scour the world—
you have the ground sense necessary.

See! the hearse leads.
I begin with a design for a hearse.
For Christ's sake not black—
nor white either—and not polished!
Let it be weathered—like a farm wagon—
with gilt wheels (this could be
applied fresh at small expense)
or no wheels at all:
a rough dray to drag over the ground.

Knock the glass out!.
My God—glass, my townspeople!
For what purpose? Is it for the dead
to look out or for us to see
how well he is housed or to see
the flowers, or the lack of them—
or what?
To keep the rain and snow from him?
He will have a heavier rain soon:
pebbles and dirt and what not.
Let there be no glass—
and no upholstery, phew!
and no little brass rollers
and small easy wheels on the bottom—
my townspeople what are you thinking of?

A rough plain hearse then
with gilt wheels and no top at all.
On this the coffin lies
by its own weight.

                No wreaths please—
especially no hot house flowers.
Some common memento is better,
something he prized and is known by:
his old clothes—a few books perhaps—
God knows what! You realize
how we are about these things
my townspeople—
something will be found—anything
even flowers if he had come to that.
So much for the hearse.

For heaven's sake though see to the driver!
Take off the silk hat! In fact
that's no place at all for him—
up there unceremoniously
dragging our friend out to his own dignity!
Bring him down—bring him down!
Low and inconspicuous! I'd not have him ride
on the wagon at all—damn him—
the undertaker's understrapper!
Let him hold the reins
and walk at the side
and inconspicuously too!

Then briefly as to yourselves:
Walk behind—as they do in France,
seventh class, or if you ride
Hell take curtains! Go with some show

of inconvenience; sit openly—
to the weather as to grief.

Or do you think you can shut grief in?
What—from us? We who have perhaps
nothing to lose? Share with us
share with us—it will be money
in your pockets.
                    Go now
I think you are ready?

Moira Linehan (1945–)

ARS POETICA

Nine-tenths preparation, this artist's work.
First, fabric between thumb and forefinger,
feeling weight, texture, give, nap. The planning
beforehand. Washing washable textiles

to shrink them before they're sewn. Laying out
the pattern so the design flows, the plaid lines
match, the dress drapes. Shears sharp so the seams
won't pucker, twist, ravel. A seamstress's stress.

Then the fitting, the pinning and re-pinning
those seams. Right shade of thread? The sewing,
seemingly magic, not one stitch visible.
Each seam, steam-pressed flat till at last the sewn

carries material and a dressmaker's vision
out into the world, all in one piece, seamlessly.

Olav H. Hauge (1908–1994)

DON'T COME TO ME WITH THE ENTIRE TRUTH

Don't come to me with the entire truth.
Don't bring the ocean if I feel thirsty,
nor heaven if I ask for light;
but bring a hint, some dew, a particle,
as birds carry drops away from a lake,
and the wind a grain of salt.

Translated from the Norwegian by Robert Bly

Mahmoud Darwish (1941–2008)

DON'T WRITE HISTORY AS POETRY

Don't write history as poetry, because the weapon is
the historian. And the historian doesn't get fever
chills when he names his victims, and doesn't listen
to the guitar's rendition. And history is the dailiness
of weapons prescribed upon our bodies. "The
intelligent genius is the mighty one." And history
has no compassion that we can long for our
beginning, and no intention that we can know what's ahead
and what's behind...and it has no rest stops
by the railroad tracks for us to bury the dead, for us to look
toward what time has done to us over there, and what
we've done to time. As if we were of it and outside it.
History is not logical or intuitive that we can break
what is left of our myth about happy times,
nor is it a myth that we can accept our dwelling at the doors
of judgment day. It is in us and outside us...and a mad
repetition, from the catapult to the nuclear thunder.
Aimlessly we make it and it makes us...Perhaps
history wasn't born as we desired, because
the Human Being never existed?
Philosophers and artists passed through there...
and the poets wrote down the dailiness of their purple flowers
then passed through there...and the poor believed
in sayings about paradise and waited there...
and gods came to rescue nature from our divinity
and passed through there. And history has no
time for contemplation, history has no mirror
and no bare face. It is unreal reality
or unfanciful fancy, so don't write it.
Don't write it, don't write it as poetry!

Translated from the Arabic by Fady Joudah

Gonzalo Rojas (1916–2011)

DON'T PLAGIARIZE POUND

Don't plagiarize Pound, don't plagiarize Ezra the marvellous
plagiarist; let him write his mass in Persian, in Aramaic, in Sanskrit,
with his half-learned Chinese, his translucent Greek
from the dictionary, his scraps of Latin, his blurred
freehand Mediterranean, his ninety-year-old artifice
of making and remaking till gropingly arriving at the grand Palimpest
     of the One;
do not judge him by the fragmentation; he had to put the atoms together,
weave them, from visible to invisible, in the fleeting warp
and the unmoving cords; let him go free
to see in his blindness, to see once more, because that's the verb: to see,
and that the Spirit, the unattained
and burning, what we truly love
and what loves us, if we are Son of Man
and of Woman, the innumerable at the depth of the unnameable; no, you
     new half-Gods
of language without Logos, of hysteria, apprentices
of the original portent, don't rob the sun
of its shadow, think of the Canto
that opens as it closes with germination, make yourselves into air,
a man of air like old Ez, who always walked in danger, leap intrepid
from the vowels to the stars, the bow
of contradiction bent to all velocities of the possible, air and more air
now and forever, before
and after the ultraviolet
of the simultaneous
explosion, instantaneous
spin, because this blinking world will bleed,
will leap from its mortal axis, and goodbye
fecund traditions of marble and light, and arrogance; laugh at Ezra
and his wrinkles, laugh from now to then, but don't steal from him, laugh,
weightless

generations, going and coming like dust, pullulating
intellectuals, laugh and laugh at Pound
with his Tower of Babel on his back like a warning of that Other
who came with his tongue;
                    the Canto,
O men of little faith, think of the Canto.

Translated from the Spanish by John Oliver Simon

Carlos Drummond de Andrade (1902–1987)

IN SEARCH OF POETRY

Don't write poems about what happened.
Birth and death don't exist for poetry.
Life, next to it, is a static sun
giving off no warmth or light.
Affinities, birthdays, and personal incidents don't count.
Don't write poetry with the body,
the noble, complete, and comfortable body, inimical to lyrical effusions.
Your drop of bile, your joyful grin, your frown of pain in the dark
are irrelevant.
Don't tell me your feelings,
which exploit ambiguity and take the long way around.
What you think and feel is not yet poetry.

Don't sing about your city, leave it in peace.
Poetry's song is not the clacking of machines or the secrets of houses.
It's not music heard in passing, not the rumble of ocean on streets
near the breaking foam.
Its song is not nature
or humans in society.
Rain and night, fatigue and hope, mean nothing to it.
Poetry (don't extract poetry from things)
elides subject and object.

Don't dramatize, don't invoke,
don't inquire. Don't waste time lying.
Don't get cross.
Your ivory yacht, your diamond shoe,
your mazurkas and superstitions, your family skeletons
all vanish in the curve of time, they're worthless.

Don't reconstruct
your gloomy, long-buried childhood.
Don't shift back and forth between
the mirror and your fading memory.
What faded wasn't poetry.
What shattered wasn't crystal.

Soundlessly enter the kingdom of words.
The poems are there, waiting to be written.
Though paralyzed, they don't despair,
their virgin surfaces are cool and calm.
Look at them: tongue-tied, alone, in the dictionary state.
Spend time with your poems before you write them.
Be patient, if they're obscure. Calm, if they provoke you.
Wait for each one to take shape and reach perfection
with its power of language
and its power of silence.
Don't force the poem to break out of Umbo.
Don't pick up the poem that fell to the ground.
Don't fawn on the poem. Accept it
as it will accept its definitive, concentrated form
in space.

Move closer and consider the words.
Each one
hides a thousand faces under its poker face
and asks you, without caring how poor or formidable
your answer might be:
Did you bring the key?

Attention:
destitute of melody and concept,
words have taken refuge in the night.
Still damp and heavy with sleep,
they roll in a rough river and transform into disdain.

Translated from the Portuguese by Richard Zenith

John Yau (1950–)

IN THE KINGDOM OF POETRY
(after Carlos Drummond de Andrade)

Don't write poems
about yourself.

Don't call attention
to your revelations

or make confessions.
Even if your intention

is to expiate pain,
overcome guilt,

temper your
understandable anger,

don't excavate
your mother's grief,

brother's sexual torment,
sister's thievery,

father's self-hatred,
step-parent's fortuitous star chart.

Feelings are not poems.
Relatives should be left

where they are found,
in the gutter

or by a cash register.
Don't write poems

about others.
Leave out husbands,

divorcees, alcoholics,
pimply adolescents, and nurses.

There is already a surplus
of bad movie scripts.

Forget about friends
and enemies,

anniversaries
and special moments.

Someone in the greeting card business
has already covered these topics.

Don't write about
what is happening in the world,

the missing child
and the human remains,

the burning beach
and the swallowed page,

the president's
fiftieth speech.

Whatever happened there
isn't a poem.

Don't try and prove
how sensitive you are.

Others have already
claimed to be plants.

It isn't necessary to demonstrate
how insensitive you are

as this is already
an indisputable fact.

Don't write poems
linking

an ordinary event
in your life

—shaving, adjusting your bra, riding subway,
admiring especially picturesque sunset—

to a significant moment in history
—pogrom, starvation, exile, assassination—

or to a myth—rape, jealousy, or rejection—
in fact to anything that has a theme.

Poems are not papers
delivered at conferences.

Don't sing about the joys of the city
or list the virtues of rural life.

Don't mention swans,
bologna, eyeball dryness,

or one-eared philosophers.
Picnics and paintings are not poems.

Don't resort to drama
or telling lies.

Don't use your yearning
as a starting point.

Secrets should be left
where they are.

Don't stand up
in a burning theater

and announce,
"no one listens to poetry."

Don't write poems
about poets

being underpaid.
Throw away

your memories,
bury your mirrors.

Louise Erdrich (1954–   )

ADVICE TO MYSELF

Leave the dishes.
Let the celery rot in the bottom drawer of the refrigerator
and an earthen scum harden on the kitchen floor:
Leave the black crumbs in the bottom of the toaster:
Throw the black cracked bowl out and don't patch the cup.
Don't patch anything. Don't mend. Buy safety pins.
Don't even sew on a button.
Let the wind have its way, then the earth
that invades as dust and then the dead
foaming up in gray rolls underneath the couch.
Talk to them. Tell them they are welcome.
Don't keep all the pieces of the puzzles
or the doll's shiny shoes in pairs, don't worry
who uses whose toothbrush or if anything
matches, at all.
Except one word to another. Or a thought.
Pursue the authentic—decide first
what is authentic,
then go after it with all your heart.
Your heart, that place
you don't even think of cleaning out.
That closet stuffed with savage mementos.
Don't sort the paper clips from screws from saved baby teeth
or worry if we're eating cereal for dinner
again. Don't answer the telephone, ever,
or weep over anything that breaks.
Pink molds will grow within those sealed cartons
in the refrigerator. Accept new forms of life
and talk to the dead
who drift in through the screened windows, who collect
patiently on the tops of food jars and books.
Recycle the mail, don't read it, don't read anything

except what destroys
the insulation between yourself and your experience
or what pulls down or what strikes at or what shatters
this ruse you call necessity.

Betty Adcock (1938–   )

ARS POETICA ON AN ISLAND IN THE CYCLADES

Silence is part of what I want, but only
part. Too easy an exit, silence
collapses inward, can be nothing but posing,
another blind door heavy as irony.

       When words come
they should wear belief sheer
as a pair of wings, serious as the silver
on the underside of olive leaves
in April wind.

       Even the thyme
on the mountain utters a fragrance
meant to be known, and the goat
cries out his fear of becoming
a stone—all things are longing,
like lost children, for a path
as if through the rubble of war
(a path that is only the breath
and the music of breath),
a way back to themselves enlivened,
aghast, unrepentant, spoken anew.

Even that which crouches lifeless:
mineral or granite or empty seashell
desires to enter memory, given voice
even if only for the length of a syllable.

       My wish is to finish
with poems pale as their paper, to begin
with the letter A, to leave
nothing out.

That wish is formless, is only
a hope borne swaying on a boat
to one of the circle of islands flowering
on blue shawls of Aegean sky.
I bring with me a history
to be shredded like a poppy in the winds
of an older place. May I be so perfectly
torn as to come back with an alphabet
of shadows spilling
                          where falls the sun.

Marianne Boruch (1950–   )

THE ART OF POETRY

isn't sleep. Isn't the clock's steady
one and one and one though seconds eventually make
an hour. And morning passes
into a thing it might not recognize by afternoon.

Or you practice the ordinary art
of shrinking strangers back to children, who they
could have been: bangs straight across,
boys and girls the same.
I blink kids into grown-ups too, who they
might be, the exaggerated gestures we do,
the weight on each word
a warning, kindly
or just so full of ourselves
we can't help it. But this oddest

not old or young, male, female,
this century or that—it simply
visits. This who, this
what. This art
of suspension. Wait.

If you've ever acted, you understand what it is,
standing in the wings, the dark
murmur out there. Every dream
for days you nightmare that. Saying or not saying.
Then wake to lights, the other
pretenders on stage bowing, happy enough.
Except it's not

like that, this wish
being small: to make emptiness
an occasion, the art of calling it down.
To wonder for the first time as I *write it.* And elegant
is good. And story. And edgy
half-uttered in fragments is good. Always that
sense of the dead overhearing. Or simply: voice I never,
not once in the world, give me a sign.
I'll pick up the thread. Dally with it, sit in its coma,
wait for its news in the little room
off the nurses' station. Don't be

maudlin, says the garden, don't
be pretty pretty pretty, and don't think whimsy
unto irony disguises.
Because it is
a garden. You walk and walk and twilight now,
its darker half
half-floats a yellow still visible in high spiky things.

There's a dovecote where nothing nests. There's an expanse
orderly as blueprint but flowers get wily, only
make believe they agree the best place
to stand or lean. It's not the sun.
I can't decide anything. Can't decide.

Begging bowl, ask
until asking is a stain. Every garden's a mess.
Am I poised at an angle? Am I listening?
A stillness so
different than winter's, lush and forgetful though

all the lost summers lie in it. Old photographs,
children a century ago who

never thought to leave still busy
fading into sepia, making houses in the yard out of
porch chairs tipped over,
and sheets. Their worn shirts, their hair every
which way. Someone loved them.
She raised a camera.

But I don't,
don't mean that. It's the art of the makeshift
almost house. Or how the children
don't see her, so aren't
dear yet.

Carolyn Forché (1950–   )

PRAYER

Begin again among the poorest, moments off, in another time and place.
Belongings gathered in the last hour, visible invisible:
Tin spoon, teacup, tremble of tray, carpet hanging from sorrow's balcony.
Say goodbye to everything. With a wave of your hand, gesture to all you
      have known.
Begin with bread torn from bread, beans given to the hungriest, a carcass
      of flies.
Take the polished stillness from a locked church, prayer notes left between
      stones.
Answer them and hoist in your net voices from the troubled hours.
Sleep only when the least among them sleeps, and then only until the birds.
Make the flatbed truck your time and place. Make the least daily wage
      your value.
Language will rise then like language from the mouth of a still river. No
      one's mouth.
Bring night to your imaginings. Bring the darkest passage of your holy book.

Keki N. Daruwalla (1937–   )

ON A BED OF RICE

If there is terror without
and you huddled in the coils
that define your being
it is best to stay
within your writer's block;
lie there long-haired one
in the cool consoling dark,
twirling the silver bracelet
studded with stones, around
the lustrous brown of your wrists

the walls will dream for you
your glass bangles will speak in the voice
that has got lost in the cavern of your throat
and time and hope will tick
till both get lost in each other,
time fatigued and bored with this endless replication
like rain repeating itself nightlong on a tiled roof

but can someone tell you,
pursed lip, starched dhoti
and shawl dripping from his shoulder
in a waterfall of silk,
to stay within, that region
where light itself turns rickety
as it navigates the smudged glass?
can he ask you to lie there
soundless, your chords un-strummed
numb and immobile?

2

that's where they want you
and how they want you
a cold roast
on a bed of rice.

3

can you write in the dark
won't thought and word balk at scribbling on the walls,
the same glass walls through which
light gets a tremor
as it navigates the outer rim of reality?
move out of the dark doorway and the blind alley
there are no dead ends,
the planet wide enough for all;
reach out for the open
with your words, but words
will never be enough;
song and slogan and gesture,
make them your friends,
and the clenched fist.

4

and the one who tinkers
with the baroque arabesques of the Zodiac
and slots you in squares
tilted water pot and the
stupid Murakami sheep—forget him.
bustle out of the square into the plaza
don't let them move you back
in rococo time.

5

don't worry about the time to come
and the time gone.
aren't the past and the future
all the same
just pages to write upon?

Blaga Dimitrova (1922–2003)

ARS POETICA

Write each of your poems
as if it were your last.
In this century, saturated with strontium,
charged with terrorism,
flying with supersonic speed,
death comes with terrifying suddenness.
Send each of your words
like a last letter before execution,
a call carved on a prison wall.
You have no right to lie,
no right to play pretty little games.
You simply won't have time
to correct your mistakes.
Write each of your poems,
tersely, mercilessly,
with blood—as if it were your last.

Translated from the Bulgarian by Ludmilla G. Popova-Wightman

Martín Espada (1957–   )

BARBARIC YAWP BIG NOISE BLUES
for David Lenson

The Professor played saxophone for the Reprobate Blues Band,
rocking the horn like an unrepentant sinner at the poet's wedding.
I was the best man, and the band howled at my punch lines about
the president while the bride's family made Republican faces at me.
Later, in the dark, The Professor passed a joint to the harp player,
remembering a thousand gigs in the firefly-light of the reefer,
a night of saxophone delirium with John Lee Hooker, who broke
a string on his guitar and chanted *Boogie with the Hook.*

That was before the poet caught his wife at Foxwoods Casino
gambling away the rent money. That was before the harp player
hanged himself from the tree in his front yard. That was before
the stroke blacked out the luminous city in The Professor's brain.

I tracked him down at the nursing home on a hill hidden from the town.
He labored to drop the jigsaw puzzle pieces of words into the empty
spaces. The label on the door said *door;* the label on the bed said *bed;*
the label on the window said *window.* The saxophone was a brass
question mark leaning in the corner, blues improvisation banned
by the nurses to keep the patients drowsing in sedation and soup.
The man with the white beard two doors down was born in 1819,
 said The Professor. *You mean 1918,* I said, unscrambling the code.

I escorted him to the picnic table in the middle of the parking lot,
slipping Whitman's *Leaves* from my back pocket like contraband.
The Professor saw the face on the cover, and the words cranked
the wheels of his jaw: *I. Celebrate. Myself.* Blues improvisation
broke out in the parking lot. I would read and he would riff:
Yes. Right. Fantastic. I read: *I am the man, I suffer'd, I was there.*
The Professor whispered: *How does he know?* as if the bearded

seer in the poems could see him sitting at the picnic table.
I read: *I sound my barbaric yawp over the roofs of the world.*
The Professor heard a band so loud the neighbors called the cops.
That's what I need, he said. *I can't make that big noise for myself.*

I left The Professor at the nursing home on the hill. I left Whitman too.
Tonight, the label on the door says *yawp.* The label on the bed says *yawp.*
The label on the window says *yawp.* The Professor swings on his saxophone
in the parking lot, oblivious to the security guards who rush to tackle him,
horn honking like a great arrowhead of geese in the sky: *Yawp. Yawp. Yawp.*

Yusef Komunyakaa (1947–   )

BLUE LIGHT LOUNGE SUTRA
FOR THE PERFORMANCE POETS
AT HAROLD PARK HOTEL

the need gotta be
so deep words can't
answer simple questions
all night long notes
stumble off the tongue
& color the air indigo
so deep fragments of gut
& flesh cling to the song
you gotta get into it
so deep salt crystalizes on eyelashes
the need gotta be
so deep you can vomit up ghosts
& not feel broken
till you are no more
than a half ounce of gold
in painful brightness
you gotta get into it
blow that saxophone
so deep all the sex & dope in this world
can't erase your need
to howl against the sky
the need gotta be
so deep you can't
just wiggle your hips
& rise up out of it
chaos in the cosmos
modern man in the pepperpot
you gotta get hooked
into every hungry groove

so deep the bomb locked
in rust opens like a fist
into it into it so deep
rhythm is pre-memory
the need gotta be basic
animal need to see
& know the terror
we are made of honey
cause if you wanna dance
this boogie be ready
to let the devil use your head
for a drum

lucille clifton (1936–2010)

study the masters

like my aunt timmie.
it was her iron,
or one like hers,
that smoothed the sheets
the master poet slept on.
home or hotel, what matters is
he lay himself down on her handiwork
and dreamed,   she dreamed too,   words:
some cherokee, some masai and some
huge and particular as hope.
if you had heard her
chanting as she ironed
you would understand form and line
and discipline and order and
america.

Robert Bly (1926–   )

THE GAIETY OF FORM

How sweet to weight the line with all these vowels!
Body, Thomas, the codfish's psalm. The gaiety
Of form lies in the labor of its playfulness.
The chosen vowel reappears like the evening star
Westerly, in the solemn return the astronomers love.
It comforts us, says: "I am here, be calm."
When a vowel returns three times, then it becomes
A note; and the whole stanza turns to music.

Quincy Troupe (1939–   )

WHAT THE POETIC LINE HOLDS

the line can be taut as a straight clothesline
strung across a patch of field full of sun-
flowers, a whip in the hand of a lion-tamer,
cracking out commands, a geometric groove between
two points, straight as an arrow flies true to the target,
like a flat jump shot leaving the hands of michael
jordan, with the game on the line, a ruled line,
upon which sets a string of words perched
like a flock of blackbirds gossiping high
up on a telephone wire, their dark shapes silhouettes
against a day sky, their black shapes holding true
forms a series of black hole seductions for our speech
to flow through, is like what improvisation does whenever
it changes up whatever is said inside & through a line like jazz
riffs, is perhaps what bird passed on to miles in an instant
of rare beauty, is what his sense of liberation was at that time
& so on & so forth, ad infinitum, on the other hand
the line can be as loose as a goose frolicking in clear water,
shaking a tailfeather baby, whatever the mind holds
true as its artistic inclination, is what the poetic line stretches
our deep limits out into, is a moment we can dive through,
find the other side & that is what possibly shapes the line,
whatever the imagination is able to manage,
hold onto, the music there following a snaking flow
of words, that act like notes embedded inside
a composition, is what the poetic line holds, clues,
perhaps a fragment, a sliver of bright sound,
glinting, as a gold tooth hit by a glancing ray of sun
can evoke a solo & so on & so forth, ad infinitum

Billy Collins (1941–   )

SONNET

All we need is fourteen lines, well, thirteen now,
and after this one just a dozen
to launch a little ship on love's storm-tossed seas,
then only ten more left like rows of beans.
How easily it goes unless you get Elizabethan
and insist the iambic bongos must be played
and rhymes positioned at the ends of lines,
one for every station of the cross.
But hang on here while we make the turn
into the final six where all will be resolved,
where longing and heartache will find an end,
where Laura will tell Petrarch to put down his pen,
take off those crazy medieval tights,
blow out the lights, and come at last to bed.

Linda Pastan (1932–   )

PROSODY 101

When they taught me that what mattered most
was not the strict iambic line goose-stepping
over the page but the variations
in that line and the tension produced
on the ear by the surprise of difference,
I understood but didn't understand
exactly, until just now, years later
in spring, with the trees already lacy
and camellias blowsy with middle age,
I looked out and saw what a cold front had done
to the garden, sweeping in like common language,
unexpected in the sensuous
extravagance of a Maryland spring.
There was a dark edge around each flower
as if it had been outlined in ink
instead of frost, and the tension I felt
between the expected and actual
was like that time I came to you, ready
to say goodbye for good, for you had been
a cold front yourself lately, and as I walked in
you laughed and lifted me up in your arms
as if I too were lacy with spring
instead of middle aged like the camellias,
and I thought: so this is Poetry!

Kim Addonizio (1954–   )

PROSODY PATHÉTIQUE

Trochees tear your heart to tatters.
Lovers leave you broken, battered.
Fuck you, fuck off: spondees. So what.
Get high. Drop dead. Who cares. Life sucks.
Dactyls are you getting boozed in your underwear,
thinking of someone who used to be there.
These are iambs: Dolor. Despair.
And going on and on about your pain,
and sleeping pills, and dark and heavy rain.
Now for the anapests: in the end, you're alone.
In the bag, in the dark; in a terrible rut.
With a smirk, in a wink, the wolves tear you apart.

Todd Boss (1968–   )

ARS POETICA

Be nimble,
be quick.

Resemble
a trick.

Be tumble,
be click.

Be bumble-
bee prick.

Remember
your work

is a flammable
wick in the

candlestick
wax of your

ache. Wake.
Be humble,

but brash.
Be gamble

and cash.
Be ramble

and crash.
Be cymbal

smash.
Don't simplify,

slash. Bash
bricks into

windows
and sample

the gash.
Be ample,

prolix.
Read Hickoks

and Glücks.
Make ruckus

and roar.
Give us

what for.

Thomas Lux (1946–2017)

RENDER, RENDER

Boil it down: feet, skin, gristle,
bones, vertebrae, heart muscle, boil
it down, skim, and boil
again, dreams, history, add them and boil
again, boil and skim
in closed cauldrons, boil your horse, his hooves,
the runned-over dog you loved, the girl
by the pencil sharpener
who looked at you, looked away,
boil that for hours, render it
down, take more from the top as more settles to the bottom,
the heavier, the denser, throw in ache
and sperm, and a bead
of sweat that slid from your armpit to your waist
as you sat stiff-backed before a test, turn up
the fire, boil and skim, boil some more, add a fever
and the virus that blinded an eye, now's the time
to add guilt and fear, throw
logs on the fire, coal, gasoline, throw
two goldfish in the pot (their swim bladders
used for "clearing"), boil and boil, render
it down and distill, concentrate
that for which there is no
other use at all, boil it down, down,
then stir it with rosewater, that
which is now one dense, fatty, scented red essence
which you smear on your lips
and go forth
to plant as many kisses upon the world
as the world can bear!

VII.
Lines Stitching Here to There

Let poetry be like a key
Opening a thousand doors.
A leaf falls; something flies by;
Let all the eye sees be created
And the soul of the listener tremble...

Vicente Huidobro
from "Ars Poetica"
translated by David M. Guss

Rebecca Seiferle (1951–   )

POETIC VOICE

Where is poetry for the people?
I asked in the bookstore. They tried to sell
me a volume of Carl Sandburg. His poetry fell
open to a "two-dollar-an-hour Wop."
I slammed it shut. Who writes a poetry
for the people? Lost in the bargain bins,
Allen the Great walked up and claimed
he spoke in his mother's voice. I saw
my old friend, Mary, with my children's names
buried in her poem among the scraps of my
old letters. Now she was working on all
her relatives from Oklahoma, trying
to render their tornado fear in poetic ellipsis,
herself the whirlwind in seven veils.
Why write poetry for the people?
W. C. Williams answered, because then
you can gawk at your neighbor's wife when she
goes out in her housecoat for the morning
news. Which many are dying for lack of.
Who is a poet for the people? "I"
said Byron. "Can't you hear the rabble
calling my name in Greece?" Neruda hid
under the table. He knew this racket,
smashing into his house, *Vox Populi.*
I looked up, I saw Linda pretending
to be Tolstoy, Amy in cranky tremolo
speaking as Keats at sixty-four, Eddie
as Plato, Heidegger, Nietzsche, even
Simone Weil. Ellen as the twenty-five
million who died of the flu. All this poetry by,
for, and of the people...I speak for her,
I speak for him, for you and you and you...

Ishmael Reed (1938–   )

BEWARE: DO NOT READ THIS POEM

tonite, *thriller* was
abt an ol woman, so vain she
surrounded her self w/
    many mirrors

It got so bad that finally she
locked herself indoors & her
whole life became the
    mirrors

one day the villagers broke
into her house, but she was too
swift for them, she disappeared
    into a mirror
each tenant who bought the house
after that, lost a loved one to
    the ol woman in the mirror:
    first a little girl
    then a young woman
    then the young woman/s husband

the hunger of this poem is legendary
it has taken in many victims
back off from this poem
it has drawn in yr feet
back off from this poem
it has drawn in yr legs
back off from this poem
it is a greedy mirror
you are into this poem, from
    the waist down

nobody can hear you can they?
this poem has had you up to here
    belch
this poem aint got no manners
you cant call out frm this poem
relax now & go w/ this poem
move & roll on to this poem

    do not resist this poem
    this poem has yr eyes
    this poem has his head
    this poem has his arms
    this poem has his fingers
    this poem has his fingertips

this poem is the reader & the
    reader this poem

statistic: the us bureau of missing persons reports
    that in 1968 over 100,000 people disappeared
    leaving no solid clues
        nor trace   only
a space   in the lives of their friends

Nikki Giovanni (1943–   )

KIDNAP POEM

ever been kidnapped
by a poet
if i were a poet
i'd kidnap you
put you in my phrases and meter
you to jones beach
or maybe coney island
or maybe just to my house
lyric you in lilacs
dash you in the rain
blend into the beach
to complement my see
play the lyre for you
ode you with my love song
anything to win you
wrap you in the red Black green
show you off to mama
yeah if i were a poet i'd kid
nap you

John Ashbery (1927–2017)

PARADOXES AND OXYMORONS

This poem is concerned with language on a very plain level.
Look at it talking to you. You look out a window
Or pretend to fidget. You have it but you don't have it.
You miss it, it misses you. You miss each other.

The poem is sad because it wants to be yours, and cannot.
What's a plain level? It is that and other things,
Bringing a system of them into play. Play?
Well, actually, yes, but I consider play to be

A deeper outside thing, a dreamed role-pattern,
As in the division of grace these long August days
Without proof. Open-ended. And before you know
It gets lost in the steam and chatter of typewriters.

It has been played once more. I think you exist only
To tease me into doing it, on your level, and then you aren't there
Or have adopted a different attitude. And the poem
Has set me softly down beside you. The poem is you.

June Jordan (1936–2002)

THESE POEMS

These poems
they are things that I do
in the dark
reaching for you
whoever you are
and
are you ready?

These words
they are stones in the water
running away

These skeletal lines
they are desperate arms for my longing and love.
I am a stranger
learning to worship the strangers
around me

whoever you are
whoever I may become.

Hayden Carruth (1921–2008)

THE IMPOSSIBLE INDISPENSABILITY
OF THE ARS POETICA

But of course the poem is not an assertion. Do you see? "When I wrote
That all my poems over the long years before I met you made you come true,
And that the poems for you since then have made you in yourself become
      more true,
I did not mean that the poems created or invented you. How many have
      foundered
In that sargasso! No, what I have been trying to say
Is that neither of the quaint immemorial views of poetry is adequate for us.
A poem is not an expression, nor is it an object. Yet it somewhat partakes of
      both. What a poem is
Is never to be known, for which I have learned to be grateful. But the aspect
      in which I see my own
Is as the act of love. The poem is a gift, a bestowal.
The poem is for us what instinct is for animals, a continuing and chiefly
      unthought corroboration of essence
(Though thought, ours and the animals', is still useful).
Why otherwise is the earliest always the most important, the formative?
      The *Iliad*, the *Odyssey*, the Book of Genesis,
These were acts of love, I mean deeply felt gestures, which continuously
      bestow upon us
What we are. And if I do not know which poem of mine
Was my earliest gift to you,
Except that it had to have been written about someone else,
Nevertheless it was the gesture accruing value to you, your essence, while you
      were still a child, and thereafter
Across all these years. And see how much
Has come from that first sonnet after our loving began, the one
That was a kiss, a gift, a bestowal. This is the paradigm of fecundity.
      I think the poem is not
Transparent, as some have said, nor a looking-glass, as some have also said,

Yet it has almost the quality of disappearance
In its cage of visibility. It disperses among the words. It is a fluidity, a vapor,
        of love.
This, the instinctual, is what caused me to write "Do you see?" instead of
        "Don't you see?" in the first line
Of this poem, this loving treatise, which is what gives away the poem
And gives it all to you.

Pattiann Rogers (1940–   )

ALL THE ELEMENTS OF THE SCENE

In the upper righthand corner of this scene is a copse
Of cottonwood (populus deltoides). Each leaf
Like a silver dollar twists on its flattened stalk.
And parallel to the edge of this scene runs
A line of forest, thin dwarf oak, scrub vine,
The smoketree. Leaning to the left of that, a field
Of flat grasses sways, heavy with thorny seeds. Blue
Toadflax and beebalm bend in the wind toward
The bare rim of the pond in the foreground, its lazy
Wash surfaced with the baweedle bug, the raised eyes
Of the leopard frog (rana pipiens). Pickerelweeds
Make hostage of the dragonfly, the nesting mud tortoise.

Here am I in this scene too, my shadow wrinkling
On the water of the pond, my footprints making pools
Along the bank. And all that I say, each word
That I give to this scene is part of the scene. The act
Of each thing identified being linked to its name
Becomes an object itself here. The bumblebee hovers
Near the bitter orange of the mallow weed. That sentence
And this one too are elements of the scene.

This poem, as real as the carp sliding in green
At the bottom of the pond, is the only object
Within the scene capable of discussing both itself
And the scene. The moist, rotting log sinks
Into earth. The pink toothwort sprouts beside it.
The poem of this scene has 34 lines.

And see, reader, you are here also, watching
As the poem speaks to you, as it points out that you
Were present at the very first word. The fact of your
Cognizance here is established as you read this sentence.
Take note of the existence of the words in this scene
As they tell you—the pond is purple; the sun is blocked
In branches below the oak; there are shadows
On this poem; night things are stirring.

Lynn Emanuel (1949–)

THEN, SUDDENLY—

> *All bad poetry springs from genuine feeling.*
> —Oscar Wilde

Yes, in the distance there is a river, a bridge,
there is a sun smeared to a rosy blur, red as
a drop of blood on a slide. Under this sun,
droves of poetry readers saunter home
almost unaware that they are unemployed.
I'm tired of the dark forest of this book
and the little trail of bread crumbs I have
to leave so readers who say *garsh* a lot
can get the hang of it and follow along.
And so I begin to erase the forest and
the trees because trees depress me, even
the idea of a tree depresses me. I also
erase the white aster of a street lamp's
drooping face; I erase a dog named Arf;
I erase four cowboys in bolas and yet in
the diminishing bustle of these streets I
nevertheless keep meeting People-I-Know.
I erase them. Now I am surrounded by
the faces of strangers which I also erase
until there is only scenery. I hate scenery.
I wind rivers back on their spools, I unplug
the bee from the socket of the honeysuckle
and the four Black Angus that just walked in
like a string quartet. "Get a life," I tell them.
"Get a life in another world, because this is
a page as bare and smooth as a bowling alley,"
and, then, suddenly—renouncing all matter—
I am gone, and all that's left is a voice, soaring,

209

invisible, disembodied, gobbling up the landscape,
an airborne cloud of selfhood giving a poetry reading
in which, Reader, I have made our paths cross!

Eavan Boland (1944–2020)

THE ORAL TRADITION

I was standing there
at the end of a reading
or a workshop or whatever,
watching people heading
out into the weather,

only half-wondering
what becomes of words,
the brisk herbs of language,
the fragrances we think we sing,
if anything.

We were left behind
in a firelit room
in which the colour scheme
crouched well down—
golds, a sort of dun

a distressed ochre—
and the sole richness was
in the suggestion of a texture
like the low flax gleam
that comes off polished leather.

Two women
were standing in shadow,
one with her back turned.
Their talk was a gesture,
an outstretched hand.

They talked to each other
and words like 'summer'
'birth' 'great-grandmother'
kept pleading with me,
urging me to follow.

'She could feel it coming'—
one of them was saying—
'all the way there,
across the fields at evening
and no one there, God help her

'and she had on a skirt
of cross-woven linen
and the little one
kept pulling at it.
It was nearly night…

(Wood hissed and split
in the open grate,
broke apart in sparks,
a windfall of light
in the room's darkness)

'…when she lay down
and gave birth to him
in an open meadow.
What a child that was
to be born without a blemish!'

It had started raining,
the windows dripping, misted.
One moment I was standing
not seeing out,
only half-listening

staring at the night; the next
without warning
I was caught by it:
the bruised summer light,
the musical sub-text

of mauve eaves on lilac
and the laburnum, past
and shadow where the lime
tree dropped its bracts
in frills of contrast

where she lay down
in vetch and linen
and lifted up her son
to the archive
they would shelter in:

the oral song
avid as superstition,
layered like an amber in
the wreck of language
and the remnants of a nation.

I was getting out
my coat, buttoning it,
shrugging up the collar.
It was bitter outside,
a real winter's night

and I had distances
ahead of me: iron miles
in trains, iron rails
repeating instances
and reasons; the wheels

singing innuendoes, hints,
outlines underneath
the surface, a sense
suddenly of truth,
its resonance.

Nikky Finney (1957–)

THE GIRLFRIEND'S TRAIN

"You write like a Black woman who's never been hit before."

I read poetry in Philly
for the first time ever.
She started walking up,
all the way, from in back
of the room.

From against the wall
she came,
big coat, boots,
eyes soft as candles
in two storms blowing.

Something she could not see
from way back there but
could clearly hear in my voice,
something she needed to know
before pouring herself back out
into the icy city night.

She came close to get a good look,
to ask me something she found
in a strange way missing
from my Black woman poetry.

Sidestepping the crowd
ignoring the book signing line,
she stood there waiting
for everyone to go, waiting
like some kind of Representative.

And when it was just the two of us
she stepped into the shoes of her words:

Hey,
    You write real soft.
    Spell it out kind.
    No bullet holes,
    No open wounds,
    In your words.
    How you do that?
    Write like you never been hit before?

But I could hardly speak,
all my breath held ransom
by her question.

I looked at her and knew:
There was a train on pause somewhere,
maybe just outside the back door
where she had stood, listening.

A train with boxcars
that she was escorting somewhere,
when she heard about the reading.

A train with boxcars
carrying broken women's bodies,
their carved up legs and bullet riddled
stomachs momentarily on pause
from moving cross country.

Women's bodies;
brown; black and blue,
laying right where coal, cars,
and cattle usually do.

She needed my answer
for herself and for them too.
Hey,
    We were just wondering
    how you made it through
    and we didn't?

    I shook my head.
    I had never thought about
    having never been hit
    and what it might have
    made me sound like.

You know how many times I been stabbed?

She raised her blouse
all the way above her breasts,
the cuts on her resembling
some kind of grotesque wallpaper.

How many women are there like you?

Then I knew for sure.

She had been sent in from the Philly cold,
by the others on the train,
to listen, stand up close,
to make me out as best she could.

She put my hand overtop hers
asked could we stand up
straight back to straight back,
measure out our differences
right then and there.

She gathered it all up,
wrote down the things she could,
remembering the rest to the trainload
of us waiting out back for answers.
Full to the brim with every age
of woman, every neighborhood
of woman, whose name
had already been forgotten.

The train blew its whistle,
she started to hurry.

I moved towards her
and we stood back to back,
her hand grazing the top
of our heads,
my hand measuring out
our same widths,
each of us recognizing
the brown woman latitudes,
the Black woman longitudes
in the other.

I turned around
held up my shirt
and brought my smooth belly
into her scarred one;
our navels pressing,
marking out some kind of new
equatorial line.

Natasha Trethewey (1966–   )

AT DUSK

At first I think she is calling a child,
my neighbor, leaning through her doorway
at dusk, street lamps just starting to hum
the backdrop of evening. Then I hear
the high-pitched wheedling we send out
to animals who know only sound, not
the meanings of our words—*here here*—
nor how they sometimes fall short.
In another yard, beyond my neighbor's
sight, the cat lifts her ears, turns first
toward the voice, then back
to the constellation of fireflies flickering
near her head. It's as if she can't decide
whether to leap over the low hedge,
the neat row of flowers, and bound
onto the porch, into the steady circle
of light, or stay where she is: luminous
possibility—all that would keep her
away from home—flitting before her.
I listen as my neighbor's voice trails off.
She's given up calling for now, left me
to imagine her inside the house waiting,
perhaps in a chair in front of the TV,
or walking around, doing small tasks;
left me to wonder that I too might lift
my voice, sure of someone out there,
send it over the lines stitching here
to there, certain the sounds I make
are enough to call someone home.

VIII.
Letters to the World

A poetry of the meaning of words
And a bond with the universe

I think there is no light in the world
But the world

And I think there is light

George Oppen
from "The Poem"

Michael Waters (1949–   )

CREATION

Vollard loved to tell his clients this story—

Degas, having arrived late for dinner,
paused with his host in the hushed, crowded parlor
—this host was a famous Parisian collector—
to view his painting recently hung there:
young ballerinas after rehearsal, sprawling backstage
or pivoted at the waist to untangle satin laces,
their hair cascading palest pinks and yellows,
exuding a weary, unself-conscious beauty.
Degas stared and stared till, without a word,
he lifted the picture in its gilt-edged frame
from its spot on the wall, the guests aghast,
then hefted it home under his arm
that he might retouch one dancer's limb.
He never returned the painting, never
passed near that gentleman's house again
while—here Vollard would clap his hands!—
all over Montmartre patrons of the arts
chained their Degas to their parlor walls.

Who hasn't been taught that a work of art
is never finished, but always "abandoned"?
Some tinker forever, souls fluttering in wrists,
allowing the light to surrender each stroke.

Imagine God's exhaustion once the earth
neared completion, before man was abandoned
to video arcades and two-story malls...
His infinite elation, the week's work gone well,

how He'd even transcended His own limitations—
then that inconsolable letdown, the probable certainty
that He could never again populate a planet
even if He took all of eternity, never again
bear to face such a vast, virginal
burnished white waste and,
beyond this, *how*

                 —the planet spinning now, luminous
as the archetypal pearl—
did He ever manage to float such a world?

Emily Warn (1953–   )

THE WORD BETWEEN THE WORLD AND GOD

Which gods gave birth to which language?
Which language gave birth to which gods?
Which gods remembered which poems?
Which poems remembered which gods?
Which memory compelled the poet to write her first poem?
Which poem compelled the poet to remember her first memory?
Which memory broke into words without effort?
Which broken words were made whole by memory?
Which memory broke all the words in all the languages?
Which word unlocks the god hidden in the world?
Which hidden world contains the word of god?
Which hidden world have I locked away without words?
Which hidden world contains the ghost of a memory too terrible for words?
Which words saved which souls?
Which souls gave which words to the world?
Which words said goodbye to which souls?
Which words are the last words?
Which words cross over the river of souls?

Who rescued herself with a word?
Who stole time for language?
Who encouraged language to steal?
Who taught language to be a sanctuary?
Who built a sanctuary out of words?
Who let herself listen to words hallowing the wind?
Who scooped out time in the quickening evening by naming an eyeful of stars?

William Stafford (1914–1993)

VOCATION

This dream the world is having about itself
includes a trace on the plains of the Oregon trail,
a groove in the grass my father showed us all
one day while meadowlarks were trying to tell
something better about to happen.

I dreamed the trace to the mountains, over the hills,
and there a girl who belonged wherever she was.
But then my mother called us back to the car:
she was afraid; she always blamed the place,
the time, anything my father planned.

Now both of my parents, the long line through the plain,
the meadowlarks, the sky, the world's whole dream
remain, and I hear him say while I stand between the two,
helpless, both of them part of me:
"Your job is to find what the world is trying to be."

Adam Zagajewski (1945–2021)

TRY TO PRAISE THE MUTILATED WORLD

Try to praise the mutilated world.
Remember June's long days,
and wild strawberries, drops of rose wine.
The nettles that methodically overgrow
the abandoned homesteads of exiles.
You must praise the mutilated world.
You watched the stylish yachts and ships;
one of them had a long trip ahead of it,
while salty oblivion awaited others.
You've seen the refugees going nowhere,
you've heard the executioners sing joyfully.
You should praise the mutilated world.
Remember the moments when we were together
in a white room and the curtain fluttered.
Return in thought to the concert where music flared.
You gathered acorns in the park in autumn
and leaves eddied over the earth's scars.
Praise the mutilated world
and the gray feather a thrush lost,
and the gentle light that strays and vanishes
and returns.

Translated from the Polish by Clare Cavanagh

Joy Harjo (1951–   )

REMEMBER

Remember the sky that you were born under,
know each of the star's stories.
Remember the moon, know who she is.
Remember the sun's birth at dawn, that is the
strongest point of time. Remember sundown
and the giving away to night.
Remember your birth, how your mother struggled
to give you form and breath. You are evidence of
her life, and her mother's, and hers.
Remember your father. He is your life, also.
Remember the earth whose skin you are:
red earth, black earth, yellow earth, white earth
brown earth, we are earth.
Remember the plants, trees, animal life who all have their
tribes, their families, their histories, too. Talk to them,
listen to them. They are alive poems.
Remember the wind. Remember her voice. She knows the
origin of this universe.
Remember you are all people and all people are you.
Remember you are this universe and this universe is you.
Remember all is in motion, is growing, is you.
Remember language comes from this.
Remember the dance language is, that life is.
Remember.

Jane Hirshfield (1953–)

FOR THE *LOBARIA, USNEA*, WITCHES HAIR, MAP LICHEN, BEARD LICHEN, GROUND LICHEN, SHIELD LICHEN

Back then, what did I know?
The names of subway lines, buses.
How long it took to walk twenty blocks.

Uptown and downtown.
Not north, not south, not you.

When I saw you, later, seaweed reefed in the air,
you were gray-green, incomprehensible, old.
What you clung to, hung from: old.
Trees looking half-dead, stones.

Marriage of fungi and algae,
chemists of air,
changers of nitrogen-unusable into nitrogen-usable.

Like those nameless ones
who kept painting, shaping, engraving
unseen, unread, unremembered.
Not caring if they were no good, if they were past it.

Rock wools, water fans, earth scale, mouse ears, dust,
ash-of-the-woods.
Transformers unvalued, uncounted.
Cell by cell, word by word, making a world they could live in.

Gregory Orr (1947–   )

from HOW BEAUTIFUL THE BELOVED

Weren't we more than
Electricity and dust?

Weren't we the hours
We lay beside
Each other?
      Weren't we

The marks
We made on the page?

Weren't we the days
We knew we had purpose
And every step
We took was praise?

*

This is what was bequeathed to us:
The earth the beloved left
And, leaving,
Left to us.

No other world
Than this one:
Willows and the river
And the factory
With its black smokestacks.

No other shore, only this bank
On which the living gather.

No meaning but what we find here.
No purpose but what we make.

That, and the beloved's clear instructions:
Turn me into song; sing me awake.

Wallace Stevens (1879–1955)

THE IDEA OF ORDER AT KEY WEST

She sang beyond the genius of the sea.
The water never formed to mind or voice,
Like a body wholly body, fluttering
It's empty sleeves; and yet its mimic motion
Made constant cry, caused constantly a cry,
That was not ours although we understood,
Inhuman, of the veritable ocean.

The sea was not a mask. No more was she.
The song and water were not medleyed sound
Even if what she sang was what she heard,
Since what she sang was uttered word by word,
It may be that in all her phrases stirred
The grinding water and the gasping wind;
But it was she and not the sea we heard.

For she was the maker of the song she sang.
The ever-hooded, tragic-gestured sea
Was merely a place by which she walked to sing.
Whose spirit is this? we said, because we knew
It was the spirit that we sought and knew
That we should ask this often as she sang.

If it was only the dark voice of the sea
That rose, or even, colored by many waves;
If it was only the outer voice of sky
And cloud, of the sunken coral water-walled,
However clear, it would have been deep air,
The heaving speech of air, a summer sound
Repeated in a summer without end.
And sound alone. But it was more than that,
More even than her voice, and ours, among

The meaningless plungings of water and the wind,
Theatrical distances, bronze shadows heaped
On high horizons, mountainous atmospheres
Of sky and sea.

                It was her voice that made
The sky acutest at its vanishing.
She measured to the hour its solitude.
She was the single artificer of the world
In which she sang. And when she sang, the sea,
Whatever self it had, became the self
That was her song, for she was the maker. Then we,
As we beheld her striding there alone,
Knew that there never was a world for her
Except the one she sang and, singing, made.

Ramon Fernandez, tell me, if you know,
Why, when the singing ended and we turned
Toward the town, tell why the glassy lights,
The lights in the fishing boats at anchor there,
As the night descended, tilting in the air,
Mastered the night and portioned out the sea,
Fixing emblazoned zones and fiery poles,
Arranging, deepening, enchanting night.

Oh! Blessed rage for order, pale Ramon,
The maker's rage to order words of the sea,
Words of the fragrant portals, dimly-starred,
And of ourselves and of our origins,
In ghostlier demarcations, keener sounds.

The Editors

Robert Hedin is the author, translator, and editor of more than two-dozen books of poetry and prose. The recipient of many honors and awards for his work, including three National Endowment for the Arts Fellowships as well as fellowships from the Bush, McKnight, and Yaddo Foundations, he has taught at the University of Alaska, the University of Minnesota, St. Olaf College, and Wake Forest University. He is co-founder (with his wife, Carolyn) and former director of the Anderson Center, a residential artist retreat in Red Wing, Minnesota.

James Lenfestey is a former college professor, administrator, and award-winning editorial writer for the *Minneapolis Star Tribune*. He is the author of the memoir, *Seeking the Cave: A Pilgrimage to Cold Mountain*, a book of personal essays, as well as seven collections of poetry. He has also edited two poetry anthologies and co-edited *Robert Bly in the World*. As a journalist, he covers education, energy policy, and climate science. He lives in Minneapolis, Minnesota.

Acknowledgments

The editors wish to express their deepest gratitude to Dennis Maloney and White Pine Press for the support and unfailing commitment to make this collection possible.

Grateful acknowledgment also to Wendy Amundson of Night Owl Graphics and Frederick Courtright of The Permissions Company, LLC, for their generous assistance in the preparation of the manuscript.

245

Index of Poets, Titles, and First Lines

263